THE HOUSE & GARDEN BOOK OF
Romantic Rooms

THE HOUSE & GARDEN BOOK OF
Romantic Rooms

ROBERT HARLING · LEONIE HIGHTON · JOHN BRIDGES

COLLINS

First published in 1985
by William Collins Sons & Co Ltd
London . Glasgow . Sydney . Toronto
Auckland . Johannesburg

Harling, Robert
The House & Garden Book of Romantic Rooms.
1. Interior decoration
I. Title   II. Highton, Leonie   III. Bridges, John

747   NK2110

ISBN 0-00-411983-5

Printed in Italy by New Interlitho, Milan

see page 36

see page 56

see page 74

see page 178

Contents

see page 104

see page 124

see page 164

see page 176

see page 196

see page 213

see page 236

see page 254

That word 'romantic'

Most of us have shared that exciting theatrical experience when the curtain rises upon the opening scene of a play and the audience utters a collective sigh of appreciation before breaking into spontaneous applause. No singer, actor or dancer is the recipient of the clapping. Instead, the set.

Sets by imaginative designers for *Der Rosenkavalier*, *The Tales of Hoffman*, *The Importance of Being Ernest*, *The Second Mrs Tanqueray* and a dozen other operas and drawing-room plays are apt to evoke such applause. So, too, is the elegant interior in *A Month in the Country* or the balcony scene in *Romeo & Juliet* in the ballet versions of those masterpieces. The theme which is common to all these sets, and which unfailingly delights the audience, is the element of romantic escapism. After all, who among us lives in cossetted comfort in a fairytale palace attended by a devoted staff? Which of us plighted a troth below a beloved's balcony? Who last spent a languorous summer afternoon blissfully involved in an exquisite *pas de deux* in a bare yet beautiful pavilion overlooking an endless blue sea? Not many, we may be sure. Little wonder, then, that we respond so fulsomely to these romantic *mises en scène*.

The art of the set-designer is not just to create an appropriate setting for the players but to heighten the theatrical fantasy for the audience, and thus the sets which receive the greatest acclaim are invariably the most resplendent or the most evocative. In many ways, the set designer's art is mirrored by that of the contemporary interior decorator. There is still an important (if declining) school of austere modernism but, compared with, say, fifteen years ago, this has been tempered by a major infusion of romanticism. Hard-edged interior 'design' has been softened by 'decoration'. Patterned wallpapers have replaced plain hessian; marbleised paint effects have enriched flat emulsion; colourful chintz has ousted oatmeal linen; pastel dhurries now overlay neutral body-carpet. The emergent, more romantic look in interiors, which is often based on reinterpretations of traditional themes and symbols, is a reaction to the blandness of modernism. Perhaps it also reflects a need for an element of richness, even frivolity, in an economic climate which urges restraint and moderation.

Yet what exactly do we mean by that word 'romantic'?

Few words in the English language seem to be more elusive of definition than this casually and widely-used term. Dictionaries tend to be ambiguous, falling back on the old lexicographical chestnut of telling us that anything 'romantic' must be possessed of the qualities of 'romance'. Mildly frustrated, we turn to the definition of 'romance', only to be referred back to the word 'romantic'.

Only in music is the romantic element defined with any degree of assurance. In the Shorter Oxford Dictionary, for example, the composer of such melodies is deemed to have 'subordinated form to theme'. Reflection confirms that this definition is eminently appropriate for most aspects of the romantic situation. Not only do most concert-goers prefer the unashamedly romantic themes of Tschaikovsky or Rachmaninov to the austere twelve-note forms of Schoenberg and Berg, but the definition also seems to apply equally well to other aspects of romance. Even humanity itself. Consider the number of so-called 'romantic attachments' in which form has undoubtedly been subordinated to theme. The chauffeur marrying the beautiful heiress daughter and so on. Sometimes with triumphantly felicitous results, of course. Sometimes disastrously. As in music, so in the rest of life. We all know how treacly

Dinner for two in a setting which could not fail to produce an aura of romance and excitement. Designed by Jean-François Daigre.

and banal some romantically-inclined music can prove.

So, too, in our houses. The *theme* in our domestic lives that is apt to dominate *form* is undoubtedly a combination of decorative individuality and comfort. Most of us want a sitting-room which, on entering for the first or thousandth time, evokes a sense of visual pleasure plus a prospect of relaxation. Most of us want a bedroom that is decorative and offers an irresistible invitation to make love or to slumber. We are not one whit concerned that the room should be an exercise in pure form as in a museum room-set in the authentic Chippendale or Bauhaus manner. We willingly forego form for the simple, but elusive, theme of comfort and aesthetics. If, in the course of that quest, we find that others consider our rooms rather romantic, then we are only too delighted to accept those civil words as an agreeable and flattering bonus. As in the finest romantic music, form and theme are unified. Indeed, we might plagiarize that sensible definition and claim that the rooms which truly delight our eyes offer us a kind of visual music.

These enquiries into definition inevitably prompt thoughts of those who seem able to design such rooms out of thin air, as if blessed by what seems to be a felicitous dispensation from the more hedonistic deities. For them, the making of romantic (or even fantasy) rooms appears effortless and natural. They are able to spin their magical webs on an economic shoestring and in the most improbable places. A tumbledown cottage; a floor in a riverside warehouse; a gutted attic . . . such unlikely settings often provide the cubic space in which they make their fantasies come true.

Backgrounds also play their part. Not only what these designer-decorators do with their walls but what Man and Nature have done beyond the windows. Almost any room in a house perched on a headland above the ocean is romantic. So is a room facing distant mountains or hills; or looking across to a lake or river, however far-off; or even, perhaps, a room overlooking the Manhattan skyline or the rooftops of Rome or Paris. The romantic appeal of these rooms, with their majestic vistas, is enhanced by the knowledge that we can enjoy Nature or Industry from a secure shelter.

But other factors are also involved. The associative qualities of culture, history and even climate are essential to our understanding of a romantic room. The kind of room which would stir the imagination of, say, an Arab potentate or Indian rajah, is appreciably different from one that appeals to an Oxbridge don or Texan oil mogul. Yet each member of that quartet might sense romantic qualities in a room evolved to suit the tastes of any one of the other trio. We can all recognise romanticism in decoration when we see it, even though we may find it difficult to define.

Part of the difficulty in defining romanticism is brought about by its abstract nature and by the subtle changes that take place in society's perception of art and decoration. One generation's view of romanticism in design will vary considerably from another's. In the eighteenth-century, for instance, classical architecture was not considered intrinsically romantic because that was the accepted style of building. 'Romantic' buildings were usually picturesque departures from the norm – gothick, perhaps, or rustic or exotic – and the historical or cultural associations they evoked were central to their appreciation.

Similarly, because the 'normal' style of building in the mid-twentieth century has been, until recently, modernism, our idea of romantic design rarely includes anything which is solely modern. Our concept does, however, embrace that which previous ages considered classical. The deliberate act of building or decorating in a classical style is sufficiently outside the twentieth-century mainstream to constitute a wilfully romantic act – just as a gothick folly in the eighteenth century was a self-conscious escape from the rational classicism of Palladianism. Indeed, modernism is usually so un-romantic that almost any departure from its influence must, in some degree, be the action of a neo-romantic. Even the post-modern movement is romantic in its references to the architectural symbols of the past.

Romantic rooms, then, come in many forms and, for that matter, themes. They may evoke the past, exploit a view, paint an illusion or, most importantly, express a mood. Perhaps the one consistent thread is a strong element of symbolism□

A pair of Delft tulipières establishes the theme in this China blue-and-white bedroom designed by David Mlinaric. The bed is romantically and extravagantly canopied with fabric printed with cherry-blossom.

The quest for the past

The history of interior decoration records frequent recurrences of nostalgia which, during the past two centuries, have spawned a succession of revivalist movements, from neo-Greek and neo-Pompeian to neo-medieval and neo-Georgian. Every generation seems to have felt the need to reinterpret the past – though never before, perhaps, on such a scale and with such enthusiasm as today. Psychologists would no doubt say that the current Western mania for surrounding ourselves with the paraphernalia of earlier times is a manifestation of our lack of belief in our own endeavours, for truly self-confident people – the first Elizabethans, the Georgians and the Victorians – were, on the whole, more concerned with the arts and artifacts of their own time than with any revival of past endeavours. For every Horace Walpole, William Morris and other eighteenth- and nineteenth-century eccentric antiquarian who entertained a belief in a never-never land of yore, thousands of more down-to-earth types preferred to take the offerings of contemporary carpenters, weavers, potters, printers and other craftsmen.

The thrusting, successful Victorian businessman had no second thoughts or sense of guilt in banishing to the attics the restrained, elegant furniture of his forebears. He preferred to fill his home with new, more ostentatious and weightier pieces which, he felt, better reflected his status. Such men were proud of being successful and keen to provide evidence of their success to all who visited their homes. The Great Exhibition of 1851 reflected the Victorians' belief in the merits of the goods they made in their own workshops and factories. And the emergent breed of new-rich, middle-class entrepeneurs and tradesmen, who liked to be encompassed by all that was new, took to the merchandise with a will. Such buoyant confidence proved profitable for architects, decorators and craftsmen in all divisions of domestic design: potters at Doulton, cabinet-makers at Maples, mattress-makers at Heal's and many, many others. With the occasional, though notable, exceptions of a few industrialists who sought to establish for themselves a spurious lineage of great length and respectability by building an 'ancestral' home, usually in the Elizabethan style, the Victorians were about the last generation to believe wholeheartedly in the politics, economics and aesthetics of their own time.

Evocations of the early nineteenth century in a room in Rome in which classical and orientalist elements are combined by Stefano Mantovani and Manuel Gimenez. Colour and scale are surprisingly (and successfully) bold for a comparatively modest space.

(Opposite) Black-and-gilt chairs by Thomas Hope and a neo-classical statue are powerful elements in this contemporary interpretation of an Antique dining-room. Designed by Thomas Kyle.

A golden Aubusson sets the tone for the drawing-room in Lady Rothermere's apartment in London. Above hangs a magnificent George III chandelier.

(Left) Rampant revivalism: early nineteenth-century models of ancient Roman ruins find renewed favour in the late twentieth century. (Right) A starred and tented Empire-style bedroom in London inspired by Malmaison in France.

The neo-classical ballroom at the British embassy in Washington, designed by Sir Edwin Lutyens in 1930, recently refurbished by John Stefanidis using traditional English chintz.

Nowadays, we are a less certain people. Two terrible wars, industrial strife and escalating manufacturing costs have sapped our belief in our superiority over the past and undermined our hope for the future. And as we all know, at times of self-doubt, a profound sub-conscious drive directs us to seek security wherever we may find that elusive state of mind and body. And the most likely place is also the nearest: home.

When we look around, those aspects in the home which spell the greatest security are apt to derive from the past, whether from the historical past or from our own more recent past. These reminders of our forebears, or even of our own childhood, give us a sense of continuity, an essential element in romantic memory.

But we are all dichotomous, even multichotomous, creatures, and such Jekyll-and-Hyde personae are clearly evident in our domestic surroundings. We may like a drawing-room which evokes that sense of serenity and carefreedom romantically associated with the age of Jane Austen – never mind that the ongoing Napoleonic wars were never mentioned in any of her books – but we do need a few equally reassuring and carefully selected notions from our own time. We prefer subdued lights, but not at the expense of filling oil-lamps. Instead, we use dimmer switches. We want warmth, but not if the whole family has to huddle round an open fire. We choose central heating. We still like to have an open fire, of course, but not if it means chopping the wood. Instead, we take the easy way out and switch on the gas-logs.

The dichotomy is seen in its most obvious form in those truly twentieth-century rooms which are power-houses of contemporary technology: the kitchen and the bathroom. The so-called 'streamlined' kitchen, which was all the rage in the nineteen-fifties and 'sixties, has been largely superseded by a much warmer, more traditional style of kitchen in which there is a deliberate attempt to make things seem more natural and human. During the past decade, many manufacturers have produced kitchens reminiscent of idealized nineteenth-century farmhouse kitchens, in which all the family gathers cosily round the scrubbed wooden table. Even that austere, horribly British institution, the ice-cold and comfortless bathroom, is continuously undergoing the same kind of soft transformation. The latest bathrooms tend to have romantically ruffled curtains and blinds, Victorian-style baths and even an upholstered armchair to give the room something of the air of a small sitting-room. We see nothing odd in opting for contemporary design for our creature comforts and decoration from the past for our visual pleasures.

A minority of purists sees this dichotomy as bogus and hypocritical home-making. If you live by electricity made available by modern science, why not live with the chairs and beds that modern designers and manufacturers have made available? The logic of such a contention is undeniable, but the response to the worthy pleas for contemporary patronage is apt to be luke-warm. Most of today's patrons and taste-makers tend to be more involved with designs from the past. Very few interior decorators specializing in modern domestic interiors have achieved the kind of international influence and patronage vouchsafed to a decorator such as Geoffrey Bennison. Bennison, who died far too young in 1984, was one of the earliest of contemporary exponents of the art of using elements from the past, especially huge-scale objects, unusual furniture and splendid antique textiles, to produce supremely lush and vigorous interiors. His style has been emulated by a whole school of decorators and antique dealers who latched on to the deceptively simple idea that beautiful things of all eras will live happily together, and that once-beautiful things remain beautiful, maybe becoming even more so as they decay. 'Shabby Chic', as the look has been dubbed, has become very chic indeed.

Decay brought about by age and loving use has almost become a virtue in its own right, and there are conscious efforts by owners and decorators to create rooms which look old before their time. If decorators cannot find the exact piece of antique furniture or fabric they need, they will resort to having a new piece made and then cunningly 'aged' until it looks as though it had existed for a century or more. Such simulating is a reflection of the widespread wish to establish roots and an ancestry for ourselves, and it is a look which shows few signs of abating. Also symptomatic of our times is that such renowned interior decorators as David Mlinaric and François Catroux who, in the 'sixties, flirted with modern design, have moved on – if that is not a contradiction in terms – to designing with a strong feeling for the past. (Another well-known interior designer who started out in the modern idiom has even described his current style as a romantic version of 'Italian palazzo'.) It is not just that the particular taste of these practitioners has gone that way, but that taste in general has turned against modernism. For many people, modernism has proved too cold, too unsympathetic – too unromantic, depriving would-be decorators of the luxury of enjoying decoration for decoration's sake.

The human spirit has always responded to pattern and decoration, whether in a drawing on a cavern wall or in a beautiful printed paper on a domestic wall. If good decoration is not available, then bad decoration will suffice – at least for the majority. And due to a lengthy period in this century in which decoration was frowned upon by modern architects – those self-appointed arbiters of taste – home lovers who unashamedly preferred decoration, and for whom variations upon pale geometrics on paler backgrounds seemed excessively unexciting, were forced back to the past. Whether that past was the comparatively recent William Morris or the more distant Chippendale and Robert Adam, was wholly dependent on personal preference. The main thing was

Family portraits and Louis XVI chairs are paired across a rusticated corner in a house in Belgravia. Between, a handsome Regency table and urn.

A nineteenth-century glazed gothic bookcase and a print alcove with seventeenth-century Dutch cabinet in a room of Soanian red and green evoke a dilettante's cabinet of the 1840s. Arranged by Stephen Calloway.

A pedimented Kentian overmantel and vigorous cornice establish eighteenth-century elegance at Ston Easton Park in Somerset, restored by Peter and Christine Smedley assisted by David Brian and Jean Munro.

Twentieth-century classicism: a recent scheme by Charles Hammond revitalized the drawing-room of an early-nineteenth-century house in London.

Symmetry, harmony and unusual wall finishes in a two-room apartment decorated by Michael Newhouse. At left, an arrangement set against felt-covered walls and, at right, against painted peg-board.

Radiating inlaid marble floor and a pair of classical terms recessed in alcoves in the oval hall of Lady Rothermere's flat in London.

(Opposite) Reminders of Louis XIV: stately French furniture in a setting of rugged grandeur. Designed by Jacques Garcia.

that the past seemed to offer such inexhaustible riches. Travellers to those far-off times were, and are, invariably surprised and delighted by their discoveries and rediscoveries.

Those who are seized by this passion-for-period syndrome are, happily, in for a lifetime's hobby. They may make themselves broke, but decorative nostalgia seems to ignore all rational values. Extravagant prices are paid for historical pieces. The contents of Elveden Hall in Suffolk were sold through Christie's in 1984 for over six million pounds sterling. This sum included such costly items as a pair of Georgian armchairs at over £45,000; a pair of lacquer cabinets (over £80,000); and a Louis XIV Gobelin tapestry (over £90,000). And so on and on. These astonishing figures reflect how much we now value the past, but the true collector will always nurture the romantic belief that such glorious objects will turn up, covered in dust, in a junk shop for next to nothing.

Sometimes, the romantic lure of the past is connected as much with the historical associations of particular pieces of furniture, paintings and objects, as it is with their intrinsic beauty. The study on page 17 is a case in point. This was designed as a tribute to Napoleon; a visual tribute collected and cherished by a true connoisseur and enthusiast for that period. On one wall hangs a portrait of Napoleon in coronation robes, painted by Gerard in 1809. Under this imposing piece stands a large desk made in 1813 to Napoleon's instructions by the Italian maker, Luigi Manetti. This is appropriately partnered by a desk-chair heavily decorated with ormolu. Made by Jacob Frères, it once stood in the Emperor's study at Malmaison. In the window bay is a magnificent *Empire* bed, now used as a sofa, which is the twin of one at Fontainebleau. The walls of the room are lined with Napoleonic documents, artifacts and objects, while the library includes several hundred biographies of Napoleon as well as those of notable contemporaries.

The current obsession with revivalism is apt to go well beyond selecting individual objects for schemes of interior decoration. We suspect that our forebears had a closer acquaintance than ourselves with the art of assembling these manifold elements into a *mise en scène* sponsoring incomparable visual pleasure and we seek to emulate not just their taste in single pieces but in creating comprehensively evocative moods. Today's most imaginative decorators are less bothered by the value or correctness of individual pieces in the room as by the overall effect. For them, the whole is far greater than the parts. 'The Look' is what they are after. Brian Juhos, for example, has made a delightful, traditional sitting-room in a tiny attic flat in Bayswater, and, in many ways, it symbolizes a golden age in interior decoration – albeit on a much-reduced scale. Although such an interior (page 32) is loosely evocative of the early decades of the nineteenth century, it is quite different in feeling from rooms decorated in, say, the 1920s and 1950s, which also

Regency furniture and ruffled windows in a delightfully confected blue-and-white supper-room arranged by Thomas Kyle.

(Left) A drawing-room in Sussex decorated by Sabine de Mirbeck and Tricia Guild using a 'distressed' cream paint finish as a background for fine antiques. (Right) Even bathrooms are now being decorated with a strong feeling of nostalgia. This one in London, with its patterned paper and dark woodwork, has something of the look of a Victorian sitting-room.

A George I-style winged chair is decorous fireside seating in an elegant Virginian sitting-room furnished mainly in the eighteenth-century manner.

(Opposite) In a room of imperial associations, Napoleon is shown in coronation robes and surrounded by a cluster of Napoleonic prints and documents. The furniture, too, recalls the Empire.

sought to capture an early spirit, and it could never have existed before the present day. To contemporary eyes untrained in the history of decoration, Brian Juhos' decoration may seem to echo the antique look, but to future historians researching the latter half of the twentieth century, the room will undoubtedly have many, and obvious, indicators revealing its true date. Not just the sofas and matching chair, which are patently of our own time, but the way in which the room's components are combined, and even the choice of components reflects a particular age and taste. The room on page 36, decorated by Stephen Calloway, is more elusive to assess because the twentieth century seems to have been banished altogether. Yet, paradoxically, that very discipline is just what may suggest its 1980s date.

That there is a renewed interest in neo-classicism is clear to all who browse through magazines and books devoted to interior decoration: it can even be detected, much simplified, in some modern furniture and post-modern architecture. This direction is seen in many rooms in this book, including two sitting-rooms designed by Adriano Magistretti and shown on pages 26 and 40. In the first, the designer-decorator has exploited the room's curved ceiling by painting it to simulate sky in the traditional manner. He has then lined the walls with a family of patterned fabrics. Finally, he has used magnificent antique furniture and objects, many in the neo-classical style, to produce a room which is truly original yet full of romantic associations with the glorious days of the *Empire*.

In the second room designed by Magistretti, a yearning for the richness and authority of neo-classicism has been satisfied within a post-war building which was devoid of architectural interest but is now a treasure-house of classical antiquity. Another structure which is not as antique as it seems is the yellow drawing-room on page 18. Despite the mature appearance, the architecture is less than thirty years old.

The enjoyable thing about playing with past styles is the enormous scope offered to the self-indulgent decorator, who can be both purist and pasticheur, recreating the perfect eighteenth-century room in the style of Robert Adam, or selecting from several centuries of design and decoration and arranging the various elements in an entirely new manner.

The strand which runs through all these evocations is the wish to be reminded of all that is agreeable and exciting from the past. We can blot out unpleasant thoughts and reflect romantically on all those earlier generations who have sat round a newly-acquired Regency dining-table. We can speculate on who has previously owned and cherished the Minton urn that now sits so proudly on the chimneypiece. We can paint a mind's-eye portrait of the one who commissioned the idyllic landscape painting that we chanced upon so happily in a country auction□

In pursuit of the eighteenth century

The most surprising thing about this handsomely proportioned drawing-room in the South Downlands of Sussex is that, in spite of the venerable appearance, it was built within the last thirty years. The architect responsible for the room, constructed as a pavilion-like extension to a late eighteenth/early nineteenth-century house, was the renowned neo-Georgian, Raymond Erith. His client, Ian Askew, is a noted connoisseur and collector of fine art and antiques, and he has decorated the room with a deliberately eighteenth-century feeling, a style of decoration which just pre-dates the building of the original house. The yellow-striped wallpaper is finished at the corners, chair-rail and cornice with gold beading, a device traditionally used in rooms where the walls were lined with fabric. The curtain treatments are a combination of festoons and full-length drapes held back at high level. Raymond Erith chose the plaster moulding for the ceiling which, by chance, echoes the pattern of the English carpet. The neo-classical, statutory marble chimneypiece is thought to have come from one of the Pantile houses in Tunbridge Wells.

A confident gallery

This is the kind of room that could only belong to a collector with supreme confidence in his own taste. He knows exactly what pleases him in the way of objects and interior decoration, and is never influenced by outside opinion. The apartment, which is in a small seventeenth-century *palazzo* in Rome, is cluttered with recollections of past eras and personalities, but the overall impression is of the middle decades of the nineteenth century. On the pale-wood, Charles X commode stands a group of obelisks and a painted terracotta bust of a classical woman. She is just one of a crowd of two- and three-dimensional faces peering at each other across the rich kaleidoscope of reds, oranges and pinks. Holding everything together is the powerfully striped wallpaper reproduced from a remnant found in a Roman *atelier*.

The 'old French look'

Pale grey was chosen for this studio on the top floor of an 1890s mansion block in West London because it provides a pleasing background for work as well as relaxation. It also evokes what the pioneer American decorator, Elsie de Wolfe, characterised at the turn of the century as 'the old French look'. The powerful architectural quality of the room, with its handsome round-headed studio window, is underscored by furniture of many different styles and dates, but each chosen for its good lines. The aim has not been to create a room of any one period but to evince a feeling for the past by association. The predominant theme is neo-classical, and this is seen in the plaques by the great nineteenth-century Danish sculptor, Bertel Thorvaldsen, which hang to either side of the marbleised chimneypiece as well as in the two plaster sculptures of the 1880s which flank the opening to the dining-area. The latter is decorated in the manner of an early nineteenth-century print-room, using black-and-white engravings, again mainly of neo-classical subjects, within decorative printed borders. Although having a somewhat severe style of decoration, the room is softened by restrained ribbons and bows from which are hung the plaques; by the tassels on the chair squabs; and by the silk shawl which hangs in diaphanous folds on the wall at left.

Detailed approach to decoration

This sitting-room in Pennsylvania is a virtuoso performance using a limited range of colours with an extensive variety of period furniture and objects.

Although the room exudes a feeling for the past, there is nothing faded or fusty about it. There is a pleasing liveliness about the place, mainly derived from the owner's assurance in mixing pieces of different provenance. English and French furniture is partnered by French chandeliers (still lit by candles and not converted to electricity), painted Italian wall-panels and a Russian dancing bear. Because the room is very large, it has been broken up into several seating-areas, rather in the manner of a grand, nineteenth-century drawing-room. Some are grouped by the windows and others around occasional tables. The winter seating-area is focussed on the open fire, in front of which is a

magnificent Aubusson rug. The small-paned windows are not curtained but have festooned pelmets which continue down the sides in long, soft folds. Textile details, such as the deep fringes on the tablecloths, ribbon pattern on the carpet and silk coverings to the chandelier chains, all contribute to the room's romantic ambience. The room belongs to Thomas Kyle who is not only a knowledgeable collector but is also a talented and instinctive interior decorator. He divides his life between Europe and the States, and one of the reasons he chose his hundred-acre farm in Pennsylvania was because it reminded him of parts of England and France, in both of which countries he has spent much time. The refurbishment of his house in America has been an abiding passion in which he has been aided by Jerome Murray, a long-time friend and successful designer.

Neo-classical reinterpreted

Parioli is one of Rome's prestigious residential quarters, with many fine *palazzi* and period houses. Most of these have now been divided into apartments, and the interesting shapes of the interiors resulting from these conversions readily lend themselves to imaginative schemes of decoration. The resolute, theatrical use of colour, pattern, grand furniture and *objets d'art*, especially those with an *Empire* or neo-classical feel, not only suits these spaces but is very much in keeping with the current direction of interior design. A talented exponent of this assured style is Adriano Magistretti, whose design practice is based in Rome and New York. Here, in Parioli, the shallow curved

ceiling in a multi-functional living-room has been painted sky-blue with puffing white clouds. Magistretti wanted the ceiling to be in total contrast to the patterned walls, but, at the same time, to look appropriate with the room's architecture. The room comprises three distinct areas – sitting-area, study (not illustrated) and dining-area – all of which are decorated with variants of the same family of flower-print fabric. The windows are screened by sliding panels instead of curtains and these, too, are covered with fabric. The room is certainly no pastiche of the *Empire* manner, but it has all the grandeur and magnificence of the early nineteenth-century, while being entirely of our own time.

A vivid background for bold furniture

Next to the main sitting-room of photographer Henry Clarke's flat in Paris are the two interconnecting rooms shown here: a small sitting-area and a library, separated by an arched opening with a columned architrave in simulated *bois clair*. The walls of both rooms are covered in red self-striped fabric, a splendidly warm background for the red patterned carpet and daybed. Two steel Directoire chairs and a pouffe in the library are upholstered to co-ordinate with the fur rug and the armchair in the sitting-area. Red fabric is swagged along the wall behind the bed – a simple and stylish device echoing the neo-classical rooms of the *Empire*.

Not as casual as it seems

Marie-Louise de Persan is a leading French fashion stylist whose courtyard *pied à terre* in Paris reflects her adept way of making interior decoration seem effortless and uncalculated. She describes her taste as baroque and eclectic, with a special preference for the eighteenth-century and the nineteenth-century period of Napoleon III. She likes over-furnishing and an abundance of pictures and objects, especially things that relate to the garden outside, with the result that her flat is always packed with visual interest, and the distinction between indoors and outdoors is agreeably blurred. She also likes to play with extremes of colour, material, form and period: French oil lamps dating from 1900 live alongside eighteenth-century Chinese celadon vases now converted for lighting. Likewise, Langlois gilt-framed armchairs covered in tapestry stand near Napoleon III armchairs. It takes talent and perception to bring off such a careless-seeming medley.

Harking back to a golden age

The success of this attic sitting-room in Bayswater derives mainly from the upending of conventional views on scale. Unintimidated by the room's small floor area and low ceiling height, Brian Juhos has deliberately gone for furniture and objects of extravagant size and bold form. The walls are a pretty shade of apricot, chosen to match the flamboyant paper border which is printed with swagged fabric and festooned roses. The ceiling, door-surround and walls below the dado-rail are grey – an unconventional choice for a small room but richer and more individual than white. Within this very charming framework, Brian Juhos has assembled some good

antiques (mainly of the late eighteenth and early nineteenth century) and some pieces which have been disguised to look better than they really are. The mirror, for instance, is brand-new and originally had a brash gold finish. Now that it has been painted off-white, it is far more unusual and less obviously reproduction. The low table in the foreground is also new but it has been skilfully painted to simulate an exotic wood. The stylishly striped lampshades are also worth noting: once plain white, they have now been painted with panels in two tints of grey. The room is a delightful, almost sentimental, harking-back to a golden age of decoration.

Reciprocal influences in design

This room is difficult to pinpoint: is it Continental or could it be English? The quandary is hardly surprising because the room is in a maisonette in a typical Victorian house in Kensington, London, but the owner-decorator, Sévérine de Tonnac, is Swiss.

She had always wanted her drawing-room to be pale and light and predominantly pink, with occasional touches of other colours, and she likes pale wood furniture, which is possibly why the room conveys an almost Beidermeier air. Some of the wood is simulated to fit in with the overall scheme. The commode, for example, which can just be seen at left in the main picture, was painted dark green when discovered in a junk shop. *Trompe l'oeil* artist, André Dubreuil, painted it to imitate pale wood and decorated it with neo-classical motifs.

The chimneypiece, too, has been painted to bring back the original marble effect. When Sévérine de Tonnac took over the flat, the Victorian fireplace was in very bad condition and had to be reconstructed. Matching slabs of marble were inserted where the originals were missing, and pieces of ornamentation which had fallen off were glued back into position. The result was a bit of a patchwork, so André Dubreuil marbleised the entire surface.

The window treatment, too, had proved a problem because the bay is very large for the size of the room. Mrs Foiret of Alistair Colvin, the London firm of interior decorators, came up with the design which combines plain and flowered chintz in pink and reds for the pelmet and curtains, plain netting with a fan edge and blinds behind.

Between period room and stage-set

Stephen Calloway's academic researches into taste and style in interior decoration have inevitably influenced the way he arranges his own home. An obsession with certain period styles and a fascination with revivals mean that the rooms in his flat in a nineteenth-century stucco terrace near London's Portobello Road are full of historical allusions. But period furniture, pictures and objects become just the starting point for some imaginative leaps across the dividing line between period room and stage-set, viewing one age through the eyes of another.

Thus the black-and-white library-bedroom (page 38) is predominantly seventeenth-century in feel but seen, as it were, through the looking-glass of the nineteen-sixties. By contrast, the drawing-room shown here, filled almost entirely with early nineteenth-century things, is intended to evoke at once the charm and *stimmung* of the Biedermeier period and the chic of Vogue Regency.

The entire decorative treatment of the room began with the spectacular set of Lyons silk curtains in brilliant Empire green with huge gold medallions. These

were found in a London street market (for the princely sum of £4.00) and research has since shown that they were woven for Windsor Castle for the state visit of Napoleon III and Eugenie in 1855.

The colours of the room are bold and vibrant. A scheme of pinkish-lilac, acid-yellow, crimson and Empire green sounds impossible but somehow works. In fact, one look at the wonderful aquatint plates in Ackermann's *Repository of the Arts* reveals that vivid combinations of colours are the key to the real spirit of Empire and Regency interiors.

A cabinet of curiosities

The library-bedroom of Stephen Calloway's flat is intended to have an antiquarian flavour, evoking the cabinets of curiosities of the seventeenth-century. The black-and-white scheme centres on the Antwerp ebony cabinet of about 1650 flanked by a pair of stylish English William and Mary high-backed chairs. Above hang an Italian looking-glass in an inlaid ebony and ivory frame and portrait engravings and drawings in ebony frames of the period. The chimneypiece has been made up from pieces of rather mixed dates but includes some carving of about 1720. Panelled-in is a late version of Allessandro Allori's *Judith and Holofernes*, which echoes some of the more bizarre and macabre curiosities displayed in the cabinet. The room is seen at its prettiest lit by candles in a pair of elaborate silvered sconces in the manner of Daniel Marot. The style of the late seventeenth-century master is also suggested by the bed with panaches of ostrich feathers in urns and by the curtains with Petersham bows. The drapery of the bed is a modern fabric.

From nondescript to neo-classical

Adriano Magistretti designed this sitting-room in Rome for a collector of art and antiques. The client's particular enthusiasm for the neo-classical style provided the designer with his weighty decorative theme.

The apartment is in a post-war building lacking architectural interest and light. Adriano Magistretti had the walls scumbled, then waxed, a treatment which gives the room a luminous quality. The grey-green withstands the richness around it without detracting from the furniture and objects. The cornice and pilasters, installed to give the room an illusion of greater height and importance, are treated in a deeper shade of blue-green. Neo-classical paintings depicting scenes and personae of antiquity are close-hung on the walls, while *bassorilievi* of Roman emperors, which hang above the magnificent bureau, are juxtaposed with classical busts and fragments of Roman sculptures on table tops. There is no shortage of furniture: in all, the room has five tables and eight stools, upholstered in a rich combination of red velvet and red-and-gold silk brocade. Pale-gold brocade covers the armchairs and red-and-gold is repeated on the couch with unusual swagged back in the small library area. The pale blue-and-gold fabric on the sofa was chosen to lighten the scheme – 'to make the room seem a little less heavy and imposing', explains the designer. Cushions are tapestry on silk in colours which pick up the glowing reds, pinks and golds of the fine Savonnerie carpets.

The whole ingenious and richly decorative exercise belies the comparatively modern – and modest – architecture of the original room.

Joyous and unexpected

Behind too many Georgian elevations lie interiors which are decorated in a way which is either too 'safe', and thus dull, or are unsympathetic to the architecture. Not so in this case, a fine English manor-house, seven bays wide, with pedimented stone façade overlooking an extensive garden. Before the second world war, the house was bought by an American who set about a thorough programme of renovation, with the eminent neo-Georgian architect, Clough Williams-Ellis, as consultant. Twenty-five years ago, the house was redecorated by Colefax and

Fowler. The most recent redecorations were based on the latter scheme, with some of the original Colefax and Fowler introductions being retained.

The drawing-room is a joyous confection of pink and white, a colour-scheme inspired by the beautiful Aubusson carpet. The upholstery is in a variety of related shades and patterns, but the most decorative features of all are the rococo pelmet crestings and plaster 'frames' to the pier glasses. Altogether, an uplifting room combining unexpected colour and modern comfort with an appropriate feeling for the past.

A traditional re-arrangement

The arrangement of this room in a Victorian block in London responds to the need for comfort and space for present-day living and entertaining, yet it is sympathetic to the fine period furniture. When the owner, an international art dealer, took on the flat there was little structural work to do – but a good deal of reorganization and redecoration. Chimneypieces which had been removed by earlier occupants were replaced; the doors connecting the sitting-room, study and dining-room were re-aligned *enfilade* (see below); the walls were stippled; skirtings and cornices were marbleised, and doors were woodgrained.

Unlike many owners of traditionally-furnished rooms, the owner-designer of this interior was against the familiar pairing of sofas at right-angles to the fireplace. That disposition, he felt, would cut the room in two and provide little in the way of seating for large parties. Instead, he had made two buttoned sofa-units which are set against the walls. Additional seating is provided by a pair of giltwood chairs and a giltwood sofa, all George II period, plus a velvet-covered trefoil pouffe. To either side of the door leading to the study is a pair of William Kent mirrors, while two circular tables with long cloths conceal speakers. The handsome eighteenth-century English carpet, with its compartmented floral design on a black background, is let into a surround of grey carpeting.

The pleasures of illusion

Most cynically-minded observers of the human scene would doubtless affirm that all romantic leanings are based on illusions, and that such illusions are invariably destructive.

But not all. Especially those illusions inseparable from the visual arts – and, to a lesser degree, the performing arts. In these two divisions of the arts, the makers of illusions are constructivists for whom a calculated attempt to deceive and confuse is essential to the emotional response they wish to elicit. This artful deception heightens the audience's enjoyment by encouraging a suspension of belief in reality – hence the complexities of plot in so-called romantic plays and operas. The playwright, librettist and/or composer knowingly sets the scene for the romantic encounter, confrontation or *dénouement*, manipulating the emotions of the onlooker and bringing about the desired reaction.

In much the same way, an architect or interior decorator can skilfully set a scene for a desired effect. We are less concerned here with those many aristocrats and plutocrats who, from the eighteenth to the twentieth centuries, have had a romantic fondness (or weakness) for battlements and towers, and set about commissioning the building of mock-castles to fit their preoccupation with their idealised vision of the glories of the past. That such domestic buildings would never have to face the prospect of battering-rams or even bows and arrows was beside the point. Romantic illusion was the *raison d'être*. Whether the castle was one of those many Irish indulgences – Lismore, Gormanston, Glin and a hundred others – or, more recently, William Burges' Castel Coch in Wales and Sir Edwin Lutyens' Castle Drogo in Devon, their owners all shared one splendid self-indulgence: illusion on the grand scale. To get the full effect, of course, the beholder was required to venture into the outside world and look back at the ancient-seeming stronghold. Only thus could the full quality of the romantic illusion be appreciated: the crenellated silhouette against the sunset, the evocation of the heroic past, the thought of those surging attacks and the bravest of the brave defending.

But not many of us can commission a castle, however historically inclined our dreams. How much more cosy and instant to indulge our particular fancies and fantasies two-dimensionally and have the walls of our home, no

The Tuscan view opening, unexpectedly, off a swimming-pool in a house in central London was commissioned by Robert and Hettie Elgood to remind them of earlier years spent in Florence. It was painted by Janet Shearer.

Bedroom painted by Jean Pierre Rio using traditional fresco techniques, the design inspired by the decoration of the Casa dei Griffi in Rome.

(Opposite) Gothick gazebo tricked out with gothick decoration and make-believe view along a garden path. Painted by Lincoln Taber.

matter how modest, contain our illusions, no matter how grandiose.

Which is where the prowess of the *trompe l'oeil* artist can prove so valuable. Whether you live in a splendid apartment or a tiny bedsitter in the heart of a great city, your romantic aspirations for rural escapism can be given full scope on your walls – and, unlike so many romantic dreams, these will not fade away. They will await you, still as bright, in the morning.

And if by some other chance you live in a downland cottage or upland mansion in deeply wooded country-side, but would like a view of the sea, then why not? Why not enjoy a year-round view of a summer's seascape at the other end of the sitting-room? No problem. The choice is yours, whether for a Mediterranean bay with a small fishing-village and lighthouse below a distant headland; or the blue waters of the Indian Ocean lapping some distant coral strand; or a dhow making a slow passage south to Zanzibar ... all are attainable through the skilfull brushwork of the illusionist.

On a purely practical level, *trompe-l'oeil* can also be a useful tool for improving a room's shape, proportions and character. One fine example illustrated here, is Graham Rust's painted ceiling in the oak drawing-room at Mawley Hall in Shropshire (pages 51-53). During the recent programme of restoration at Mawley Hall, the owners commissioned the allegorical painting to echo the existing eighteenth-century over-door paintings and to counter the room's potentially heavy appearance. The artist's theme, *Paradise Regained*, was inspired by the restoration of the house and uses an architectural framework of false-perspective walls, simulating a courtyard, above which is a celestial scene of cupids frolicking with ropes of flowers. The painting also includes personal references to the family living at Mawley Hall. The whole *oeuvre* is romantic in theme and execution, yet still achieves the requirement of lightening the room's character. The false perspective leads the eye upwards and suggests a far greater ceiling height than in fact is the case.

Another instance in which *trompe-l'oeil* has been used to solve a decoration problem is the staircase painted by Ian Cairnie and shown at left. The idea of commissioning the mural came about because the staircase, though an attractive space architecturally, had proved difficult to decorate in more conventional ways: pictures could not be hung against the curved walls, and the area was too high for drops of wallpaper. When Ian Cairnie was aked to provide a solution, he immediately foresaw problems with an uninterrupted landscape mural – 'whichever way you looked at it, the horizon line would have been wrong, either sloping or simply unnatural' – and thus he devised an alternative which uses the space to the full by exploiting rather than avoiding the height and nar-rowness of the staircase. Downstairs, in the hall, the walls are painted with formal stonework. As the visitor

A woodland shelter used for shooting parties sports a teasing bar in trompe l'oeil *by Lincoln Taber for John Joliffe Tufnell.*

(Left) Bedroom in Essex with Italianate vistas and painted drapery by Lincoln Taber for John Joliffe Tufnell. (Right) A blackamoor with a tray of fruit and glass held high is a welcoming addition to a hall, painted by Ian Cairnie. The stairway of the same house is shown opposite.

Walls painted by Monica Pitman to simulate massive stonework convert a London staircase-hall into a majestic cavern. On the floor: real York paving.

(Opposite) A continuous panorama of rolling countryside and fairytale architecture solved a decoration problem in a house in London: the stairway was too high for drops of wallpaper, and the curved walls made picture-hanging impossible. Painted by Ian Cairnie.

(Left) An ordinary hall in Paris has become an impressive classical composition, thanks to bold architectural marbleising by Allamarvot-Soulier for Elie Garzouzi. (Right) Dining-room with 'dhurrie rug' stencilled on the floorboards, designed by Red Shively who is head of the interior decorating-designing firm, Gawcie.

A floor-to-ceiling window and a mural of similar proportions give a double outlook in a holiday apartment by the Mediterranean. The ceiling is tented with harmonizing blue-and-white fabric. Designer-decorator: 'Barbara'.

(Left) Fifteenth-century Italian Renaissance painting inspired the mural for the New Roman Health Spa in Bath, painted by Jackie Harding. (Right) The 'tortoiseshell' paint finish seems peculiarly appropriate to the shape of this supper room in Beverly Hills, decorated by Diana Phipps for Gore Vidal.

(Opposite) Walls in false perspective and a celestial view transform a plain, flat ceiling into a magnificent canopy of allegorical deception, also shown overleaf. Painted by Graham Rust.

rounds the first curve of the stairway, this stonework gives way to picturesque ruins and distant panoramas with a castle of fairytale outline. In the foreground, a rope is looped from tree to tree and, above, a striped awning continues the outdoor fantasy. The awning was not planned from the start, but gradually it became obvious to artist and client that something was needed to bridge the awkward junction of wall and ceiling. The stripes give the stairway the illusion of width, and the *trompe l'oeil* peak running down the centre of the awning enhances the three-dimensional effect.

Currently, the wish to create an idyllic landscape seems to be paralleled by an awareness of classical architecture, and many contemporary murals combine these two themes. Thomas Kyle, whose house in Pennsylvania must be the ideal of all romantics, has taken the sublime illusion to the limits. His hall (page 58) has been painted with a series of vistas of the quintessential English landscape garden of the eighteenth century framed by massive classical stonework arches.

In Lincoln Taber's painting of the inside of a garden pavilion in Wales designed by Simon Birch for I.O. Chance (page 46), the architectural style is gothick rather than classical. *Trompe-l'oeil* quatrefoils and a ribbed ceiling surmount stone-like walls pierced by pointed-arched doors. Some of the doors are real but the cleverest seemingly opens onto a path with a delightful herbaceous border which blooms all year round. On the make-believe ledge stands a tempting glass of wine.

But such visual illusions and delusions need not be exlusively evocative of places and objects that mean much to you. The recent revival of interest in decorative paint finishes, which have become more popular in the last decade than ever before, has meant that many a modest sitting-room has been agreeably aggrandized by the addition of a marbleised door-case or chimneypiece in siena or *verde antico* to choice. And all those workaday white doors can easily be grained to a beguiling shade of maplewood or mahogany.

Marbleising is the key to the imposed grandeur in the small Roman dining-room shown on page 54, while François Catroux has used illusion on two planes in the flat he decorated in Paris (page 62). The walls have been marbleised in an exuberant and stylised manner, which brings a sense of flamboyance to a room of good, though unremarkable, architecture, and the carpet has been woven to simulate a marble floor.

Future generations of social historians will no doubt see this fad for faking as a form of pretentiousness in the character of the late twentieth-century, but a more likely explanation is the wish for individuality in an age of mass-production. By using decorative paintwork, our rooms can be quite different from those of our friends and neighbours. These finishes also have a sense of theatre about them, which is a welcome break from the more prosaic wallpapers□

Allegorical themes in an architectural framework

The theme of Graham Rust's heroic ceiling painting of 1979 for the oak drawing-room at Mawley Hall in Shropshire is *Paradise Regained*, a tribute to the restoration of the house by his patrons, the Galliers-Pratt family. The new ceiling, which measures 24 feet by 16 feet and, contrary to appearances, is flat, was intended to complement the existing eighteenth-century allegorical paintings set in the over-door panels and to bring to the room a greater feeling of light and height – hence the false perspective of the containing walls and the open sky above. Set against the *trompe l'oeil* walls are four statues, representing the seasons and Earth, and two elaborate cartouches containing the astrological signs of the owners, Pisces and Aquarius. Along the short walls are cornucopia overflowing with fruits. In the heavens above, cherubim frolic with garlands of wild flowers, celebrating the return of Adam and Eve to Paradise, and a Banana Palm tree, a hybrid, symbolizes the cross and Eternal Life. Opposite the Banana palm, cherubim bear up the family crest.

A brilliantly bejewelled casket

Stepping into this Roman dining-room, especially at night when the candles are lit, is like stepping into a fabulous, garagantuan jewel-casket. A gem-like sparkle seems to encompass and enlighten all things. The walls have been painted to resemble panels of antique marbles: vivid green-and-black malachite; warm earth-yellow siena; North African red; Imperial-blue lapiz lazuli. Above, the ceiling is a cornice-to-cornice, tent-like *trompe l'oeil*. From the centre of this captivating artistry a magnificent Regency black-and-gilt chandelier is suspended, a fitting partner to the Regency candelabra on the table and a source of endless flashes of brilliance which ricochet off the blue-and-gold Art Nouveau plates and tureen; off the gold consommé cups from Limoges; off the Baccarat goblets and the Bavarian champagne glasses. A splendid and highly appropriate reflection of the English owner's taste, for Anthony Allen is a collector and dealer specializing in fine art, paintings and sculpture, and partner in Rome's noted Medusa Gallery.

Stepping over a fantasy

Nancy Young, the owner-decorator of this roof-top room in Knightsbridge, London, is an inveterate traveller-collector whose journeys have taken her to Thailand, Bali, Iran, Turkey and many other countries in the Far East and Middle East. Whenever she returns from these exotic visits she brings back souvenirs, albeit souvenirs of a very superior nature, and enjoys incorporating them in the decoration of her home. Even the pale Etruscan colour of the walls owes something to these travels and *objets trouvés*, for it was inspired by her collection of ancient pieces of terracotta.

But these are all very real reminders of distant lands. The floor is pure illusion. Although Nancy Young has a number of oriental rugs, mainly kilims, she wanted the fantasy of a great painted carpet covering the entire room. She commissioned Graham Carr to realize this romantic idea and, in the process, found herself becoming his assistant. The stylised pattern is a vivid underpinning to the room's most dominant piece of furniture, the campaign bed – and therein lies another romantic story. Some years ago, Nancy Young found for sale in Paris a campaign bed which was thought to have belonged to Napoleon and which, predictably, was exorbitantly expensive. Whilst she was doing up this apartment she was driving along the Fulham Road in London and saw a box in a junk shop which was exactly the same as the box which had housed the original bed, and it turned out to be the same bed – or one quite indistinguishable. Every collector will understand the thrill of making such a happy and unexpected find.

Translated landscapes

Stonework arches revealing idyllic blue skies and romantic English views create the illusion of an open-sided folly or colonnade. In reality, this is the entrance-hall to a country house in Bucks County, USA, belonging to Thomas B. Kyle, who spent over thirty years in England and France before returning to the States to seek his ideal house. With the assistance of American designer, Jerome F. Murray, and French artist, André Dubreuil, he has completely transformed his new home, bringing to it a distinctly English character, which is seen most effectively in these murals in the hall. Within a framework of flamboyant architectural paintwork are scenes of the quintessential English landscape garden of the eighteenth century: a Palladian bridge to the left of the chimneypiece and, further left still, the Temple of the Winds derived from that at Castle Howard in Yorkshire. The stairway continues the sublime illusion with a soaring arch, flower-filled urn and a delicately-wrought birdcage. And all about are hints of picturesque decay.

A neo-Greek ante-room in Mayfair

Alan Dodd's transformation of the entrance-hall of a London townhouse into a neo-Greek ante-room of pastel colours and classical motifs is a lyrical exposition of the art of deception. The vaulted ceiling, fluted pilasters and fretted frieze have such vigour and substance that it is astonishing to discover that all are illusory. Even the enriched doors and window shutters have been carved by dexterous brushwork. The pedimented overmantel, looking for all the world like a bas-relief carved in stone, is a double deceit. Not only is the classically-posed figure two-dimensional but the ragged crack at top-left is an artful device to add a touch of picturesque decay while correcting a minor discrepancy in the alignment of the chimneypiece. Only the alcoves seen to either side of the chimneypiece are real.

Altogether, a delightful demonstration of the artist's ability to create something that is scholarly yet lighthearted.

'Marble' walls and 'marble' floor

This sitting-room by the renowned French decorator, François Catroux, is on the first floor of an eighteenth-century house in Paris. It is modest in size yet has been infused with a feeling of classical grandeur by the exuberantly marbleised walls and by the use of fine objects, exquisite fabrics and, perhaps most important of all, by the symmetrical arrangement of furniture and accessories. The windows and facing doors are curtained to match; a double-sided sofa is set in the centre of the room; a pair of pictures of architectural subjects flanks the chimneypiece with its garniture of early nineteenth-century architectural models and a clock of the same period. The room is a contemporary interpretation of the classical spirit, a theme continued by the carpet which was specially woven to a design by François Catroux and simulates marble.

The mysterious East

Because the Far East (romantic enough description in itself) was for so long so remote from Europeans, the history and the arts of those ancient lands became, in time, a major interest of Western historians and art students. Those interests show no signs of declining. Indeed, never before has the West been so intrigued by Eastern culture – hence the increasing number of tourists from Europe and the United States to Japan, China, Thailand and India. Hence, too, the spectacular success of *The Jewel in the Crown* and other television and feature films which are set against an Indian background.

The first major flowering of Eastern forms in Western architecture and decoration was in the eighteenth century when the European vogue for Chinoiserie gave rise to numerous garden pagodas (one of the most impressive, designed by Sir William Chambers, still towers above Kew) and orientalist architectural detailing, such as the filigree carving of the tea-alcove and chimneypiece in the Chinese Room at Claydon House in Buckinghamshire. More long-lastingly, it resulted in the 'Chinese Chippendale' style of furniture which, even today, is extensively reproduced with varying degrees of finesse. Moghul architecture has never met with quite the same approval in the West, though there was a brief dalliance with it in the early nineteenth century when the Prince Regent built his onion-domed seaside pavilion at Brighton. The late-Victorians and Edwardians had a penchant for oriental lacquer and used Japanese forms during the Aesthetic Movement, but it was the nineteen-sixties, the Swinging Sixties, that really went overboard for the East. The hippy trail blazed a colourful path for Afghan embroideries, Madras cottons and Benares brass which make our nineteen-eighties preferences for Coromandel screens and gilded buddhas seem positively cerebral.

For over two hundred years the East has exercised a compelling spell over us, but whereas in the past Western architects and designers could only reproduce forms and objects based on descriptions from a handful of travellers who had visited those far-off regions, today thousands of Western tourists can see the real thing for themselves and even bring back authentic examples for the embellishment of their homes.

When we enter a room in which these proud borrowings from the Orient have been masterfully arranged, we are at once in a world of fantasy, splendidly and richly

This intercontinental assembly in London includes a nineteenth-century English screen with oriental scenes, a pair of Indian figures, jungle-print cushions and Eastern rug. Interior design by the Marquesa de Lavradio.

Contemporary wallpaper, handpainted in China, encircles a bedroom with traditional blossom and birds. The red lacquer table, jewellery-cabinet and faux-bamboo chair are also Chinese.

(Opposite) Lacquered walls are an appropriate background for an exotic display of eastern art and artifacts: Chinese screen and wall-hanging, lacquered table and stand, cane chairs. Designed by Peter Kuring.

(Left) Tribal jewellery collected by Henry and Tina Maier decorates the bedroom of their flat in north London. (Right) A Chinoiserie lacquered cabinet is a dark and lustrous centrepiece for a formal pairing of walnut chairs and wall sconces. Designed by Paul von Fullman.

A six-panel oriental screen and Eastern rugs provide the major input of pattern and colour in a flat in London designed by Derek Frost.

(Left) An oriental screen, lacquered sideboard and Indian figure are Eastern influences in a London dining-area designed by Lila Byoni. (Right) An eighteenth-century Coromandel screen is a handsome means of concealing the staircase in a flat decorated by Brian Juhos.

(Opposite) A Chinese wedding-bed, skilfully enlarged to suit Western scale, is raised on a dais to command a view of the skyline in couturier Dianne Benson's early twentieth-century apartment in New York.

romantic. Here is the world, we tell ourselves, that Marco Polo and those early itinerant missionaries who ventured so far into the East saw all those centuries ago: a world of ancestor portraits, lacquered screens, carved ivory and fabled silks.

Rich lustre and intense colour are inseparable from many orientalist interiors. Gold, silver, 'Chinese' reds and yellows, highly figured woods and glowing, not sombre, lacquered blacks, bring an exotic quality to a room which is rarely achieved by the chaste colours, restrained shapes and discreet graining traditionally favoured by Western decorators and cabinet-makers.

Fortunately, there does seem to be an affinity between oriental antique pieces and modern Western furniture and decoration. The exquisite screens in the flat shown on page 80 look entirely appropriate within a setting which is European and contemporary. They bring a richness to the room, yet they do not look overbearing or portentous in the way that an equivalently decorated European piece might. The felicity of this marriage of cultures derives largely from the extreme simplicity of the background. Simplicity is also the keynote in the New York bedroom shown opposite, in which plainest grey walls are a neat foil for the elaborately-carved Chinese wedding bed. Similarly, the display of the impressive collection of oriental pieces shown on page 68 is made all the more effective by the maintenance of a plain background. Here, a vast room has been decorated throughout in white to give due importance to the art and artefacts. The only modern, Western piece of furniture in the room is the huge sofa – and even this is white in order not to detract from the exotic imports. Another room in which the owner has assembled a collection of oriental pieces made during extensive travels in the East is the sitting-room on page 74 which displays a magnificent series of buddhas, their golden surfaces matched by golden mirrors, all set against an apricot background, so that the entire room shines like gilt.

Perhaps these latterday tourists who introduce oriental pieces into Western rooms are twentieth-century equivalents of the eighteenth- and nineteenth-century English milords who journeyed to Italy and Greece to 'discover' the archaeological sites of Ancient Rome and Athens. The milords became fascinated by the arts and cultures of those ancient civilizations and brought back to England classical statuary with which to decorate their halls and landscaped gardens. Its role was not only to look elegant but, more subtly, to remind the owner of his erudition and travels. There was an intellectual content over and above the obvious artistic content. Now that we are so familiar with antique Western civilizations – after all, they figure more largely than any other ancient cultures in Western school curricula, and the countries from which they sprang have been accessible for centuries – we have had to look further to satisfy our love of mystery and exoticism□

The spoils of travel

As keen and erudite collectors of oriental art, Henry and Tina Maier have furnished the forty-foot-long living-room in their flat in north London almost entirely with pieces brought back from their travels in the East. The L-shaped sofa in the more formal of the room's two seating-areas, shown at left, is the only concession to Western ideas of comfort, and even then it is played down with off-white upholstery to fuse with the colour of the walls. It presents no competition for the superb antique Thai bed which acts as a coffee-table and on which there is an ever-changing collection of oriental acquisitions. Above the sofa are works by Mark Boyle, both of which are evidently Western conceptions of art but their compositions seem surprisingly at one with the seventeenth-century Burmese buddha at right. Further right still, there is a second sitting-area, not shown, which is smaller and more casual. The dining-area (seen above) is defined by carved verandah posts and chests from Nuristan. Walls, ceiling and floor are off-white – a cool, receding background for a powerful display of exotic objects.

A splendid East–West relationship

Success in mixed marriages, whether amongst people or objects of different cultures, is notoriously difficult to achieve. But when such marriages do succeed, they are often uncommonly felicitous and make more conventional liaisons seem mundane. The daring yet triumphant contrasts occasioned by the juxtaposition of oriental and European art and furniture that characterize this duplex apartment in Paris is a case in point. The apartment was converted by Adriano Magistretti from a former artist's studio on the Left Bank, and the generous ceiling height allowed for a mezzanine floor to be inserted across one end of the room. This upper level is now a dining-room, which can just be glimpsed

through the Chinoiserie fret openings to either side of the Chinese ancestor portrait in the main photograph. The floor of the living-room has been painted brown, then subtly speckled with colour to give an interesting yet unobtrusive underpinning to the room's furnishings. Using such apparently dissonant objects all in the same room takes nerve, both on the part of the client and the designer, for how many people would place an elaborately-carved nineteenth-century, rosewood-and-marble Chinese chair alongside an eighteenth-century Portuguese desk, or a grand piano alongside an Italian Chinoiserie cabinet? Yet it all works splendidly, and even the old cast-iron columns make a spindly but decorative contribution.

Less colour, more impact

The common theme which unites architecture and soft furnishings of unmistakably Western provenance with such exotic elements as a pair of Indian silver armchairs, elaborate silver-framed Russian mirrors, a seventeenth-century inlaid ebony-and-ivory cabinet of Indo-Portuguese origin and a collection of eighteenth- and nineteenth-century Chinese bronzes, is the total lack of colour. The forms and finishes of all the immigrant pieces gain depth and intensity within the neutral surroundings. The curtains, a simple combination of sheer unlined silk next to the windows and heavy lined silk suspended from brass poles, are designed to merge with the walls, just as the travertine tables are designed to merge with the flooring. Furthermore, most of the furniture is kept very low and horizontal, which enhances the room's serene quality, and even the flowers are always chosen to harmonize rather than stand out within the decoration. Serenity was a major element in the brief to the designer, Elie Garzouzi, who was commissioned to make a room primarily for entertaining but also comfortable for day-to-day family living.

Golden reflections

A collection of beautiful seventeenth-century Japanese paper screens inspired the colour-scheme for this sitting-room in London. The deep, old-gold tones look marvellous against the sponged apricot walls. Not only that, but apricot is a perfect background for the buddhas, which include a fine tenth-century Kmer head. The statuary also embraces western works of our own time, including a bronze bust of the owner's father by the great Italian sculptor, Marino Marini, and two busts of herself by Oscar Nemon.

The room's textiles are further reminders of Eastern travels. The curtains are of Thai silk, and the sofa cushions were made from silk brought back from Japan. The exoticism of all the golden sheen of gilt and silk is emphasized by the gilt-framed mirrors and by panels of mirror which clad the chimneybreast and pier wall.

Across the continents; across the centuries

Most collectors of antiques feel compelled to display them in a traditional setting. Not so Georgio Colombari, a young antique dealer in Turin, whose flat is shown here. The inclinations and interests of a modern generation are clearly evident, but so, too, is the trained eye of the antiquarian. Everything is contrived to convey a feeling of tranquillity and to provide a neutral but sophisticated background for the fine oriental sculptures and objects. The decorative treatment of the room is kept at low level and low-key – all very horizontal, very plain. In the large window-bay is a reclining buddha in nirvana, dating from the end of the seventeenth-century. To either side of the low, lacquered podium that forms its simple but effective resting-place are two Thai bronzes of monks kneeling in prayer. These historic fourteenth-century pieces also sit serenely within their modern setting. The deep turquoise-blue Chinese rug echoes the blue of the podium and sofa cushions. White walls, carpet and Roman blinds give the impression of a blank canvas on which Georgio Colombari has painted a vivid picture of the East.

The neo-Chinoiserie

In redesigning a large, open-plan living-area, Alberto Pinto has introduced a change of floor-level and has kept the main pieces of furniture well away from the walls, bringing them into groups in the centre of the room. Thus the sitting-area, comprising three large sofas, forms an 'island' which creates a more intimate atmosphere for the sitters, yet allows plenty of circulation space around the perimeter. The dining-area is raised slightly above the rest of the room and is partially screened by a specially-designed unit with gold-plated 'pillars' for plants and smoked-glass doors concealing a television. The smaller oriental objects and patterns which appear throughout the room are presided over in the seating-area by a life-size painted Chinese figure and, in the dining-area, by portraits of Chinese emperors. The dining-chairs and low, circular table between the sofas are finished, appropriately, in deep red lacquer. The same colour reappears intermittently for cushions, lamp bases and picture mounts.

Screening the walls

Michael Reeves is a fashion consultant whose work has taken him on frequent visits to the Far East. There, his abiding interest in oriental art and decoration was encouraged, an interest which has been given tangible form in his expanding collection of exotic furniture, lacquerware and screens. In fact, it was the acquisition of two screens – each one very different and acquired separately (in London and New York) that prompted the move to this flat in Kensington. 'The screens were simply too big for where I was then living. I had no room to store them, let alone display them,' he says. One screen now embellishes the sitting-room, shown here, and the other his bedroom (shown on pages 134–135). The former is of early eighteenth-century Chinese lacquer and was originally part of a pair of six-fold screens. Two folds were rather the worse for wear, so the existing arrangement is a six-fold and four-fold screen combined. This now forms a splendid backdrop for a lacquered altar table on which rests a buddha and a pair of tea-caddies. Opposite, a temple guardian stands alongside a nineteenth-century embroidered screen.

The welcoming hearth

Scientists have solved many domestic problems and evolved many domestic amenities, but they have yet to come up with a more satisfying domestic institution than the open fire. Central heating undoubtedly gives a more pervasive warmth and a more economical distribution of available therms, but who cares about facts and figures when an open fire is the alternative on offer?

A splendid open fire has never been excelled as a romantic setting. Merely consider the number of clips from Hollywood pictures or television commercials in which the two lovers exchange meaningful looks against the background of an open fire. Curiously enough, the kind of fireplace surround or chimneypiece which frames the open fire never seems to matter overmuch, except to the decorative purist. The fire and its welcoming warmth are what we are really after. Yet for the decorator, the fire surround is one of life's most agreeable challenges. Here, relevance is all. How appalling to have a ruthlessly modern fireplace in a traditional eighteenth-century house. Almost as heinous a crime as to infiltrate a pseudo-pine, pseudo-Georgian chimneypiece into an apartment in a modern urban block. Yet does it *really* matter? Is not the welcome that the hearth transmits of much greater importance?

Only a few years ago, builders were hell-bent on tearing out the fireplaces from older houses. Now, period houses with open fireplaces are once again eagerly sought-after, and where the original chimneypieces have been removed, a new generation of home-owners is scouting around for second-hand replacements or buying reproductions. Apart from the fact that an open fire gives a significant additional source of heat and is a practical alternative if there is a power-cut, almost everyone hankers after the intimacy of sitting round a fire. Perhaps it is something to do with our collective memory going back to earliest times, for we seem unable to shake off the addiction. Even gas fires and electric fires are often designed to look like traditional hearths in imitation wood and are marketed as 'features' for interior decoration. But sitting round a gas fire can never be as pleasurable as sitting round a real fire – unless, that is, it is one of those artful gas-fuelled fires which look disconcertingly like a real coal or log fire. Gas-coal and gas-log fires have reached such sophistication that they not only look convincing but they emit a significant amount of heat. And,

This library-study, decorated by Brian Juhos, was originally two rooms – hence the twin fireplaces. The surrounds are an integral part of the pine panelling. Chintz is a fresh counterpart to the mellow woodwork.

Broad-arched alcoves with marbleised architraves flank a marble chimneypiece with ormolu mounts. The entire fireplace wall is treated as a single exercise in symmetry. Designed by Brian Juhos.

(Opposite) Lined with felt and centred on a fine marble chimneypiece, this room by Jacques Garcia is the epitome of visual and virtual warmth.

(Left) The Louis XVI chimneypiece is bold enough to hold its own in a room of heavy hues and objects, designed by Olive Sullivan. (Right) An equine theme links the painting above the fireplace with the riders on the mantelshelf. Decoration by Carrie Naylor-Leyland.

Sofas are paired to either side of the fireplace but kept well apart to avoid any sense of crowding. A pastel-coloured dhurrie acts as a link.

(Left) This highly controlled treatment of a fireplace wall revolves around a painting by Ivor Weiss: everything else is coolly subordinate. Designed by Paul von Fullman. (Right) Cheerful yet peaceful: an oak-lined library with marbleised chimneypiece, designed by Gonzalo Yanez and Lady Codrington.

(Opposite) A room of modern simplicity in which the open fireplace expresses traditional warmth. Designed by Jean de Meulder in Belgium.

for all that purists groan, there is no doubt about it: coming home in the evening and flicking a switch to get an instant 'real' fire, without the need to screw up newspaper, saw logs, hulk coal or sweep away ashes, is highly appealing in winter.

Rooms have seasonal characters. Some are 'summer' rooms and come into their own when the sun is bright, when the days are long and the weather warm. Other rooms, such as the bedroom on page 82, work best in winter. Everything within this room conspires to make the occupant feel warm and protected from the outside world. The walls are lined with felt, and the floor sports a colourful kilim. But central to the whole scheme is the marble chimneypiece with its garniture of paired busts, candlesticks and vases arranged to either side of the lacquer plaque. The mirror above is hung very low, rather in the manner of an overmantel, which allows for a picture to be hung at high level to line up with the top row of pictures to either side. The pictures and books are further contributory elements in the room's general impression of a masculine study for day-time use as well as a bedroom for the night.

A much more open character is conveyed by the pure white room opposite. Here is an interior which is obviously the work of someone who appreciates contemporary design, yet he has chosen to have an open fire as the room's focal-point. The romantic spirit lingers on – otherwise, why not settle for concealed heating? – but he has been careful to treat the chimneybreast and hearth in as simple a style as possible, in keeping with the room's decoration and furnishing. Even in a modern room, where one might have expected a television to have become the focal-point, the fire reigns supreme.

The design of fireplaces in modern rooms is a challenge which few architects and designers have satisfactorily resolved. In the old days, the surround provided a natural support for the display of decorative objects, but in a setting where ornamentation and clutter are inappropriate, the mantel-shelf no longer has a role or relevance. The contemporary answer is usually to exclude a surround altogether – though Heino Stamm, on page 100, has made a gesture towards the traditional chimneypiece.

When one goes into a traditional room without a fireplace, one is often aware that something is missing – though one cannot instantly assess what that something is. The same sensation is felt when driving along a road of neo-Georgian houses. There's something missing – but what is it? After a while, one realizes that there are no chimneys, an omission which subtly, yet dramatically, transforms the entire roofline and character of the buildings. Curiously, when young children are asked to draw a picture of a house, they nearly always include a chimney alongside the television aerial, even though they live in chimney-less houses or apartment blocks – a reflection, perhaps, of the deep and age-old significance of the open fire□

Retaining the neo-Louis embellishments

Paris, with its long tradition of flat-dwelling, has a rich stock of late-nineteenth- and early twentieth-century *appartements*. Although many of the elegant interiors have suffered in recent years the same short-sighted vandalism as their equivalents elsewhere in Europe – rooms have been sub-divided, ceilings lowered, mouldings removed, fireplaces plastered over – this turn-of-the-century example has come through to the present day with virtually all its original plasterwork intact. The owners, aware of their good fortune in having such a fine shell as the basis for their home, commissioned interior decorator Sabine Marchal to bring the flat up to scratch for contemporary living whilst maintaining all the period details. A major part of the brief was the incorporation of an important collection of French impressionist paintings.

Stepping into the light-filled *salon* from the umbrously-decorated hall is agreeably startling. Here, everything is soft and harmonic. The sympathetic interplay of grey and apricot is pretty but not cloying and gives due value to the delicately-confected mouldings. The room has two identical chimneypieces, one of which displays a pair of large, nineteenth-century Japanese bronze birds and is flanked by alcoves for porcelain. The other chimneypiece has a garniture of enormous cloisonné pots. Both displays are all the more stylish for being over-scaled.

Contrasts in time and texture

In the age of Louis XIV, conspicuous opulence was one of the main characteristics of fashionable decoration. Today, *luxe* and splendour are again important elements in traditional interiors, but the most striking examples of this new approach to historicist decoration use very grand furnishings in comparatively modest rooms without looking pretentious or ridiculous. It is a talent ably exploited by Jacques Garcia and exemplified by this sitting-room in Paris. The room is a stunning display of visual, cultural and textural contrasts: beneath rugged roof beams are highly sophisticated furniture, fabrics, carpets and decorative objects. The chimney-breast is mirrored with smoked glass framing a marble fire-surround and a magnificent ormolu bracket clock. To the right of the fireplace are a Louis XIV buhl cabinet and a series of portrait roundels. The transparent stairway, designed by Jacques Garcia, is absorbed by the richness of the surroundings.

A light-hearted restoration

What could easily have been a heavy, ponderous room has been made light and joyful, thanks to the far-sighted eye of its owner and the zestful decoration of Maurice Savinel. The room is in a venerable French chateau which, for many years, had stood abandoned and neglected. When the new owner bought the chateau, he was determined not just to restore it to what it was but to turn it into a home in keeping with the needs and spirit of our own time. The mouldings have been highlighted with two shades of pale green to echo the gentle colours of the dhurrie rug.

Chintzes bedecked with flowers and ribbons cover the sofa, chair, a pair of circular tables and even the lampshades. It is all delightfully pretty and light-hearted, with nothing old-fashioned or dark to oppress the spirit. The fire, of course, provides the essential focal-point

A change of mood

French interior decorator Serge Guen-Antin is one of the most daring of contemporary practitioners. He invites the challenge of decorative extremes – extremes of colour, age and pattern. Sometimes he will decide to decorate a room entirely in black and white; at other times he will partner medieval carvings with modern chrome. The one factor that remains constant is that he never feels intimidated by other people's rules. His eye is very much that of a designer of film-sets, for he seems able to create any number of different moods within the same cubic structure. By day, this room has a modern blue table and wire-work chairs sprayed to match. Here, the same room is arranged for an intimate fire-lit party. The columns and church ornaments remain, but the blue table has been replaced by a smaller one lavishly draped with plain, soft silk in oyster white. On top of this is a layer of gold lace. The topmost cloth is a fabulous piece of antique silk heavily embroidered with gold thread. The party chairs are equally regal: Louis XIV carved frames upholstered in white leather. The paper cornice was specially pasted up for the occasion.

Inspired by Palladio

As fast as the last generation of home-owners removed original cornices and mouldings from eighteenth- and nineteenth-century interiors, today's generation is busily putting them back. This sitting-room, not far from the King's Road in Chelsea, is Victorian in date but Georgian in its proportions. The owner is Anthony Little, founder and partner of Osborne & Little, the noted wallpaper and fabrics firm. 'Normally, I would design and decorate interiors in keeping with the date of the building,' he says, 'but, in this case, the original

layout and mouldings had been revamped and removed during the 1920s or '30s. So, freed from historical authenticity, I was able to start from the brickwork and design myself all the cornices, mouldings, fireplaces and doors – the lot, in fact.' The aesthetic theme for this total redecoration was English Palladianism, the style which Anthony Little considers the most satisfying of the classical variants. He worked closely with craftsmen joiners and plasterers, producing dozens of detailed drawings. Thus, all the architectural elements, though

classical in inspiration, are unique in execution. The discovery of a steel beam running through the wall behind the fireplace dictated the design of the bookshelves. The shelves were recessed into the wall but are surmounted by a dummy arch as it was structurally impossible to shift the beam. The broad bay is defined by a deep beam supported by Corinthian columns and pilasters. The windows, which lead onto a small balcony, are framed by curtains with deep-fringed pelmets and tails pinioned by extravagant rosettes.

Like a summer's sky

A great forsaken château
standing within its own romantic
parkland . . . this was the
irresistible challenge taken up by
a French architectural enthusiast
who has now restored the fabric
of the building and, with the help
of interior designer Maurice
Savinel, brought new life to the
interiors. All the original features
have been retained, the over-door
paintings cleaned, the cartouches
re-gilded and the chimneypiece
re-built, but this has not resulted
in a room of museum-like

formality or reconstruction.
Instead, pale colours, modern
furniture and marbleised
mouldings in heavenly shades of
blue give the room a real infusion
of 'today'. The seating is grouped
round the fire and is all low-
backed in order not to break up
the space. With the exception of
the blue sofa, white is the
dominant colour for the
upholstery. The Bonade seascape
above the chimneypiece enhances
the room's ethereal, cloud-like
quality.

A personal Vuillard

When a friend first saw Margaret Tiffin's sitting-room, she described it as her 'personal Vuillard', a reference to the room's colouring which is similar to the palette favoured by that French Intimist painter, and to the fact that Margaret Tiffin is a keen *amateur* of modern art. But such a romantic description takes little account of the basic problems that had to be overcome in decorating the room. The main difficulties were the shoe-box proportions and the lack of architectural detail. The space is very long and narrow, having originally been two rooms which a previous owner had knocked into one, and there were no cornices or mouldings to alleviate the blankness. There was, however, a good marble chimneypiece *in situ* and this has been retained as the focal-point in the sitting-area. Now, the room has been given more personality and form by the introduction of a handsome cornice, dado rail, bookshelves and broad shelf above the opening between the two halves of the room. This shelf, which is enriched by the cornice moulding, was designed to support part of a collection of oriental pots and is echoed by the shelf above the bookcase in the dining-area.

At the outset, Margaret Tiffin had hoped to decorate the walls with a hand-blocked eighteenth-century-style wallpaper but it was so expensive that she decided in favour of paint to try to achieve a similar effect. The walls were 'smudged' by artist Jackie Gyles using water-based paints, while the cornice and dado were marbleised in a deeper shade by Patricia Ludovici. The wall above the chimneypiece is faced with smoked mirror-glass which forms a backdrop for a nineteenth-century Italian gilt-framed mirror.

An undemanding background

Very few designers can resist using their own homes for experimenting with new ideas – and Heino Stamm, one of Germany's most prolific and versatile interior designers, is no exception. He lives with his family near Munich in an updated 1930s villa which, although never treated as a show-house, is inevitably used as a testing ground for furniture and lighting effects. This largely explains the near-monochrome colour-scheme in the living-room. Not only does grey provide a restful background for living but is an undemanding setting for introductions of furniture of different types and colours. Stamm's favourite colour with grey is yellow, which is seen here in the upholstery for the Louis XVI chairs at the far end of the room. Their upright form is in marked contrast with the horizontal emphasis of the velvet-covered sofa, acrylic tables and check carpet, all designed by Stamm. In a room which is so clear and geometric in execution, an over-elaborate chimneypiece would have been out of place – hence the simple surround which barely projects from the wall.

The literary retreat

The eighteenth and nineteenth centuries were marvellous centuries for well-heeled bibliophiles. Scholars, dilettantes and men of taste were all occupied with acquiring books and with housing their collections with appropriate style and distinction. Inevitably, at a time when conspicuous display was not regarded as a social misdemeanour, patricians and mercantile princes were far-from-modest in their notion of what a library should be. They prided themselves on the range of their volumes and the manner in which their intellectual interests were displayed. The libraries at the great English stately homes of Holkham, Longleat and Syon still bear witness to this pride.

The collections built up by early bibliophiles were formidable. There was, for example, the library of 16,000 volumes on natural history and travel which Sir Joseph Banks, the great explorer and naturalist, bequeathed to the British Museum in 1820. Twenty-five years later, The Hon. Thomas Grenville bequeathed his library of 20,000 rare books to the Museum. But the sheer numbers of volumes never outweighed aesthetics. Here is a contemporary description of Horace Walpole's medievalist library in his eighteenth-century gothick home at Strawberry Hill, Twickenham, Middlesex.

> The books are ranged with Gothic arches of pierced work, taken from a side-door case to the choir in Dugdale's St Paul's, the doors themselves were designed by Mr Chute. The chimneypiece is imitated from the tomb of John of Eltham, earl of Cornwall, in Westminster Abbey; the stone-work from that of Thomas duke of Clarence, at Canterbury . . . The ceiling was painted by Clermont, from Mr Walpole's design drawn out by Mr Bentley. In the middle is the shield of Walpole surrounded with the quarters borne by the family. At each end in a round is a knight on horseback, in the manner of ancient seals: . . .'

Another famous library which received equally attentive thought from its owner in every aspect of design, decoration and assembly, is in the house in Lincoln's Inn Fields, London, built for his own use by the great architect, Sir John Soane, and now the Soane Museum, one of the most fascinating museums in Britain. The architect had the unusual notion of combining library and dining-room but, as that noted bibliographical scholar, the late John Carter, once said: most disputations are apt to arise over meals and it is tidy and logical to have dictionary or cyclopaedia which will settle the matter near to hand.

A study-library in Paris with a masculine style of decoration by Sabine Marchal. The large bookcase uses the corner to advantage.

Tall, narrow bookcases flank a tall, narrow window in a library in Antwerp decorated by Axel Vervoordt. The oriental carpet provides just the right degree of pattern in a quiet setting.

(Opposite) A latterday interpretation of a traditional library in London in which the ornaments continue the historical bias: an eighteenth-century English globe; eighteenth-century Italian marble columns; English nineteenth-century copies of ancient Greek vases.

(Left) A panel of mirror recessed in the book-shelving gives a greater impression of space in this study opening onto a small courtyard in London. (Right) Bookshelves have been set in a false wall and cupboards built below to align with the dado rail – a neat and co-ordinated arrangement.

The publisher-owner of this library in London wanted a room with a club-like atmosphere – hence the large-scale mahogany bookcases with marbleised detailing. Designed by Anthony Paine.

(Left) Shelving designed by Andre Dubreuil for Severine de Tonnac frames the double doors of a library in London. (Right) Dining-rooms and book-rooms are often under-used. Combining the two, as here, is the logical and decorative solution employed by Mimi O'Connell.

(Opposite) Classical symbolism in a post-modern library in the United States designed by Charles Moore.

A contemporary visitor to Sir John Soane's house recorded his impression of the combined library and dining-room in the following portentous prose:

> The general effect of these rooms is admirable: they combine the characteristics of wealth and elegance, taste and comfort, with those especial riches which belong expressly to literature and art – to the progressive proof of human intellect and industry, given, from age to age, in those works which most decisively evince utility and power . . .Nor must we leave these rooms without giving another glance towards the enriched ceilings, which in their decorations confer an air of general grandeur and suitable completion . . .

The historical, literary and artistic allusions which were essential characteristics of the libraries of Walpole and Soane expressed an intellectual romanticism which, even now, is associated with the display of books. When we sit in a modern-day private library, we are impressed by the knowledge and culture it represents, and we have the idea that its owner is a man of letters. The impression may be false, but it is compelling nevertheless.

So what are the essential requirements of a present-day book-room possessed of 'those especial riches which belong expressly to literature'?

First and foremost, of course, you need well-designed shelving which has either been made to suit the various heights of the books or which can be finely adjusted. Then you need a desk or writing-table, a comfortable chair or sofa. Not necessarily much sunlight, though ample and efficient artificial light is essential to supplement the source of natural daylight. Overmuch sunlight does no good to books and, by association, a traditional library should not look too garish. How the books are arranged on the shelves is also important. Books look at their best if each shelf houses volumes of the same height and if there is not too much space between the tops of the books and the bottom of the shelf above. The spines of the books should also be brought in alignment to the front of the shelves. If books are pushed back against the wall, they leave depressing areas of shelving exposed at the front, which look all the worse if the books are of different dimensions.

Some of the rooms illustrated here are libraries in the full meaning of the word. The one on page 102 is a latterday interpretation of a traditional bookroom, even down to its ornaments which show an historical bias. Other rooms, however, do double-duty as sitting-rooms, but because the books are such obvious features in these rooms, they and their housing have had to be considered as integral parts of the overall decoration. The room designed by Chester Jones and shown on page 112 is a charming example of such an omni-purpose arrangement. Robert D'Ario's vivid blue room on page 116 does not house a vast number of volumes but the books are nevertheless an explicit part of the room's decoration. Note how the collection of fine tooled-and-gilded bindings is shown to advantage in the cabinet by being arranged face-on to the room□

A Gloucestershire pot-pourri

Enter the front door of Barnsley House and at once you will detect the aromatic *pot pourri* not only of log fires and flowering plants, but also the more subtle scent of erudition and cultured living. Not surprising, really, for Mr and Mrs David Verey are both immensely talented. David Verey is the author of several books, which include definitive works on *Cotswold Churches* and *Gloucester Cathedral* – both essential handbooks for would-be visitors – and *The Diary of a Cotswold*

Parson. Rosemary Verey writes for *Country Life* and has written several distinguished garden books. She is also a renowned plantswoman. Their home, Barnsley House in Gloucestershire, is built of local grey stone and looks over the now celebrated garden towards a landscape of lush meadows. The sitting-room is lined with books, and the little wallspace still visible is painted a warm terracotta, set off with blue-and-white china. Two things in this room

immediately take the eye: two 'tablescapes' but of a very different kind. One side-table, under an important eighteenth-century French portrait by Le Blond of Bordeaux, displays a collection of seeds and pods of every size, shape and shade of brown (see above); another half-moon table (not shown) is covered with dried leaves under thick glass, again of different shapes and tones – an ingenious decorative idea that is within the reach of everyone.

Decorated as a homage to Proust

This bedroom in a turn-of-the-century building in central Paris was conceived as a homage to Proust, whose person and work were enjoying renewed interest – partly due to the film *Swann in Love* – when the room's redecoration was being finalized. The literary association also appealed to Serge Guen-Antin's client who wanted to use the room as a library and study as well as a bedroom – hence the need for high-level bookshelves above the bed and the Napoleon III writing-table by the window.

The work-top seen in the photograph above was designed for working at whilst standing up, as requested by the client, and is terminated by a double-sided bookcase next to the window. The painting above the work-top is by Gaston Bertholet. The sober colours of the paintwork and textiles are combined in a vigorous manner: the écru silk bedcover is hand-painted with dark khaki diagonals; the single curtain is lavishly edged with eighteenth-century silk embroidered with gold thread. To the left of the bed is a French bronze urn (1925); to the right, an eighteenth-century Iranian teapot in cloisonné on bronze.

A zestful interior behind a 1790s façade

Unlike many libraries in eighteenth-century buildings, there is nothing dusty or forgotten about this room in a 1790s house in the imposing Place du Palais Bourbon in Paris. On the contrary, it is full of zest. Instead of predictable rows of brown-leather bindings, we see riotously-coloured modern dust-wrappers. Equally unpredictable are the audacious marbleising of the mouldings and the alternating heights of the bookcases, which were specially made to fit within the panelling. The hanging of the pictures in front of the shelves also defies convention, but at least it ensures that the owners are able to enjoy their favourite works even in a room where empty wall space is non-existent. This newly-instilled vitality is the work of Barbara Wirth and Christian Badin of the French off-shoot of David Hicks. The room, though obviously used and enjoyed by a modern family, has many associations with the past. The pictures depict Napoleonic projects for the fortification of Paris and are from a collection formed by the Duke of Wellington; the desk is of mid-nineteenth-century German Provenance; and the velvet-covered wing chair was made during the *Régence*. Even the building within which the library is housed has historical evocations, for it is said to be built of stone from the Bastille.

How to stay on the level

The disadvantage of living in a typical Georgian terraced house, with its vertical plan of only two principal rooms per floor, each with a specific function, is that the occupants are constantly having to change level. To get round the problem in a house in London, designer Chester Jones has abandoned the traditional single-use arrangement and has combined several functions all within the main living-room. Apart from the fact that the house did not offer sufficient separate rooms to cope with the varied demands of contemporary living, the new multi-purposeness of the living-room has resulted in a style of decoration which is pleasingly informal and social. Not only does the room act as a sitting-room and television room but also as a study and office – and thus the books have become an integral part of the decoration. Before

Chester Jones refurbished the house, it had been stripped of all its original architectural details, but with the agreement of neighbours, original doors, architraves and cornices were copied from adjacent houses. The bookcases were detailed to conform to the period of the room, but the painted furniture, most of which was specially designed for the client, is contemporary in spirit. The most important piece of antique furniture is the Biedermeier *bureau à cylindre*. Most of the colour in the room derives from the books, although the narrow band of pink which edges the cornice and the Roman blinds is a subtle link with the chintz upholstery. The continental fireplace had been left by a previous owner and, although not entirely appropriate to the English context, was of such good quality that it was kept.

The home of a legendary decorator

Madelaine Castaing, the most eminent of French decorators, owns a beautiful eighteenth-century house near her birthplace, Chartres, where she spends weekends and holidays. The entrance *salon* (above) is a delightful octagon with sky-painted alcoves to either side of the opening to the staircase-hall. Opening off to the right is the library which is furnished with fine English Regency pieces and has shelves designed in the Regency manner, the uprights finished with elongated capitals and gilded finials. The two rooms are linked by a carpet which is patterned to simulate leopardskin and is characteristic of a certain style of mid-twentieth-century Regency Revival, both in France and in England.

Madeleine Castaing's influence on French interior decoration began forty-five years ago when she opened a furniture shop in Montparnasse in Paris.

A moment's reflection confirms that forty-five years ago in France was scarcely the most auspicious time to take a chance and set upon a defiantly elegant shop. The city was under German occupation, and for Madeleine Castaing things could scarcely have been more unpromising and depressing. Her country house had been confiscated, and people were selling possessions rather than acquiring them. Yet that was the year when this courageous Frenchwoman decided to set up in business. From the opening day, the new boutique enjoyed an astonishing *succès d'estime*. 'People came to my shop,' she recalled, 'because I brought poetry into the home.' But she did more than evoke an escapist domestic ambience. She re-interpreted traditional decoration and was among the first French decorators to design complete room-settings for the display of the furniture she sold.

Nothing if not whole-hearted

Confidence is the name of the game in this library and adjoining study in an apartment in Bordeaux decorated by Robert D'Ario. D'Ario's approach to interior decoration is nothing if not whole-hearted. He likes strong colours and does not hesitate to use them in large quantities – as here, where royal-blue, with only the occasional relief of white, black and brown, spreads over walls, ceiling and floor. Contrary to more conventional and timid views, this designer's contention is that bold, solid colours are perfect backgrounds for paintings, period furniture and *objets d'art*. His choice of blue is undeniably imposing, and it does bring a sense of drama to a comparatively ordinary room, but a great deal depends on the skilful choice of accessories which are of sufficiently powerful character to stand up to the forceful background. The books in the wired-door cabinet have fine tooled-and-gilded bindings – hence the face-on positioning of some of the more elaborate examples. The geometric carpet, which is used in both rooms, is woven to simulate the paved floor of a Florentine *palazzo*, and it is an appropriate underpinning to the modern glass-and-chrome table as well as to the eighteenth-century armchairs.

The most romantic room?

The most surprising and significant feature about the bedroom is the inordinate time and attention devoted to its decoration when most people spend fewer waking hours in it than in any other room in the home. Perhaps this dedication derives from our subconscious recognition of the significance of the bedroom. After all, most of us are conceived in bed, make love in bed and, even in these direful times, will die in bed. To these formidable facts of life and death can be added an abundance of intervening exercises in human affection. Here we exchange our vows of undying love as well as sensual caresses. Here, too, as parents we dote upon our offspring in their earliest days. Here we reflect upon our ambitions and destinies. Not surprisingly, then, the wish to make these rooms reflective of such emotional and physical sentiment remains irresistible.

Most currently fashionable styles of decoration for the bedroom are extremely soft and feminine. Even in marital bedrooms, where one might expect the occasional concession to masuline taste, there are flowery patterns and yards of lace and frills which few men would be inclined to tolerate elsewhere in the home. One leading American decorator claims that when he works for a married couple, all the decisions about interior decoration are made by the wives and that these decisions are invariably discussed with their husbands when they are in the bedroom, thus neatly summarising the dual, and related, influences exerted by women and bedrooms on interior decoration in general.

This is partly why the bedroom is the most fascinating of rooms to analyse, for it gives away much more about its owners than the sitting-room or dining-room, both of which are designed to be seen and, to some extent, approved by outsiders. People will allow their bedrooms to indulge the sort of decoration fantasies that they would be embarrassed to acknowledge more publicly. Photographs taken at off-guard moments may be amusing souvenirs when propped up on a dressing-table, but are shameful in the sitting-room. And what about all those adults who sit teddy-bears and dolls on the bed but would shrink at the idea of bringing them into the living-room?

Just as these personal accessories explain the individual personae of the room's occupants, so the overall decoration of the bedroom is revealing of wider, more profound human needs. Very few people can resist making their bedrooms look welcoming and warm, even clut-

Bed and daybed are upholstered to match in a bedroom prettily and serenely wrapped in blue-printed cotton, which is made even prettier by inner curtains and cushions of apricot silk.

The owners of this dressing-room in London chose family tartan as a masculine foil for the adjoining bedroom which is decorated with flowers.

(Opposite) Nostalgic and summery: a country-house bedroom with late-eighteenth-century furniture and early-morning colours.

(Left) An attic bedroom in an English country house, charmingly decked out in green and white has a delicate canopy made from a onetime mosquito net. (Right) Paisley and moiré are nicely balanced for colour and richness in a London bedroom decorated by Sandra Cooke.

Continuity of colour lends tranquillity to a traditional bedroom with a carved four-poster and open fireplace. Decorated by Sabine de Mirbeck.

(Left) The ogee-shaped bed-pelmet and roped window curtains are imaginative textile treatments by Mrs John Ragsdale in her apartment in Charleston. (Right) Green and pink are lively partners in a bedroom in an eighteenth-century house in the English countryside.

(Opposite) In a bedroom in California, designed by Wayne Williamson, the sandy beige tones of the floor and walls, enlivened by touches of vivid colour on the bed, chair and decorative objects, reflect the drama and contrast of the desert hues outside.

tered, a look which has gathered momentum with astonishing rapidity during the past decade, probably as a reaction to the previous, rather unsatisfactory, period of cool modernism. Now, chintz is very much to the fore, and there has been a spectacular burgeoning of corona-style bedheads and four-poster beds. The latter must surely be the ultimate accessory to romantic escapism, for they create a totally private world within which one is cocooned from reality and need take no account of the time of day or night.

The natural 'clock' of rooms, especially of bedrooms, is interesting. Some bedrooms seem better suited to waking up in than going to sleep in, while others are just the opposite. The room shown at the opening of this chapter, on page 118, is surely in the former category, for the interplay of early-morning sunshine through the tall Georgian windows and the delicate style of decoration combine to produce an instant sense of well-being. Unlike some four-posters, which are heavy and claustrophobic, the late-eighteenth-century bed is elegant and airy. The architectural form of the frame is repeated by the *en suite* window pelmets, and the treatment of the fabric pelmets for the bed and windows is of appropriate finesse for the slim profiles of the furniture. But if the profiles are slim, the effect of the black-and-gilt finish is striking. The colours of the room, which is in a handsome eighteenth-century manor-house in Oxfordshire, are gentle and recessive, mainly pale grey-blue and cream carried through several different patterns, some new, some old.

In contrast, many bedrooms are at their most appealing during the evening, when they offer privacy and peace, a blissful interlude between dinner and bed. Sabine Marchal's enchantingly contrived room on page 150 is the perfect example of a bedroom which extends its hours of use beyond the hours of sleeping. Beside the handsome marble chimneypiece is a *chaise-longue*, an adjustable lamp and a small table – in fact, everything needed for an evening of quiet reading. The room by Carrie Naylor-Leyland on page 132 also has an open fireplace, a feature which never fails to bring a romantic aura to a prettily decorated bedroom.

Several of the bedrooms illustrated in this chapter are shown with their adjoining bathrooms because the two rooms have been designed as an entity – not necessarily using identical wallcoverings and fabrics, but with the same concept. Nina Campbell's scheme for a gallery-bedroom in a converted studio in Paris is linked with that for the bathroom by the use of co-ordinating fabrics, but the bedroom and bathroom shown on page 128 are quite different in colouring. Their mutual dependence is reflected in the owner's wish for an historical style of decoration: hence the nineteenth-century metal bath which seems a perfect complement to the grand, period-style bedroom□

The colour of ivory

Monochrome but not monotonous – a difficult feat to achieve in decoration but here successfully pulled off by Christine and Christian Ferre-Duthilleul of the Atlantide design team in France. The bedroom is decorated in a series of fabrics, all in palest off-white, which line the walls, curtain the windows and enclose the bed. The armchairs are upholstered in grey-and-white fabric to echo the pattern of the dhurrie rug. Even the decorative objects and furniture are suitably colourless: a marble bust is paired with a plaster copy on a black-lacquered table; ethnic pottery is displayed beneath a black-and-white engraving.

A small space grandly treated

Interior designer Brian Juhos has no inhibitions about using grand treatments in small spaces. His theory is that if you fill rooms with flamboyant furniture, good colours, generous curtain treatments and lots of interesting objects, there is so much to detract the eye from the smallness of the architecture that the viewer is deluded into thinking that the rooms *must* be big. After all, surely no-one would use such extravagent treatments unless he had a big space to play with?

Brian Juhos' own flat is tiny – three small attic rooms at the top of a Victorian house in a quiet square in Bayswater – and it admirably bears out the validity of the theory. In spite of the bedroom's low height, the ceiling was painted a deep coral, a wide border pasted beneath it, the bed draped with fabric from a corona, and pictures and objects massed in tight groups – all bold moves which have proved highly effective in instilling a small room with a feeling of importance.

A delicate and serene colour-scheme

This bedroom in a seventeenth-century Cotswold-stone manor-house is a country idyll realized with powdery colours, pretty chintz and an elusive wall-finish painted by Graham Carr. The room's colour-scheme was inspired by the chintz and conveys the most marvellous sense of serenity. Opening directly off the bedroom is the bathroom/dressing-room which has a blue-patterned wallpaper, edged with a co-ordinating border, and cupboard mouldings picked out in a slightly deeper tone of blue. The bathroom was the only room in the house in which structural alterations were made during the recent redecoration. The wall which divided the original bathroom from a small bedroom beyond was taken down and replaced by a waist-high partition that now conceals pipework and provides a shelf for ornaments.

Decorating with nostalgia in a Paris studio

Fin de siècle charm is exploited to
the full in the gallery-bedroom
and bathroom of a converted
artist's studio in Paris decorated
by Nina Campbell. When she
took on the project, Nina
Campbell was presented with the
bathroom more or less as it is –
with dark green walls, white
hexagonal-tiled floor, copper tub
and painted lady *in situ*. She added
the festoon blind as a cross-
reference to her choice of chintz
for the cushions and dark-red
ottoman-lined curtains in the
adjoining gallery-bedroom. As
a further cross-reference, the
curtains in the main room (seen at
right in the small picture and on
page 200) are bound with red to
pick up the red of the chintz. The
bathroom is semi-divided from
the bedroom by a glass-panelled
door.

A rooftop inspiration

The colour-scheme for this bedroom and adjoining bathroom in an early nineteenth-century townhouse in London was inspired by the view of the rooftops beyond the bathroom window. At night, the view turns peach-coloured under the effect of street lights, and designer Elaine Wilson wanted to match this effect indoors. The result is a soft peachy scumble on the walls relieved by marbleised panels. The colour is perfectly attuned to the delicate chintz chosen for the bed valance, Austrian blinds and bedside tables. At the foot of the bed, which is covered with an antique quilt and lace pillow, stands an old wooden chest. The peach-coloured marble surround to the whirlpool bath and double basin has been matched with marble tiles for the floor and bath dais. Woodwork round the bath and the cupboards below the basins were dragged and scumbled in the same colour.

Escape from the city

The style of decoration chosen for this London bedroom is a deliberate antidote to the urban setting and provides the perfect vehicle for visual escape to the country. In order to make the room look as much like a country-house bedroom as possible, the client and decorator, Carrie Naylor-Leyland, decided against putting in fitted cupboards for clothes. (These have now been installed in the adjoining bathroom/dressing-room.) For the same reason, the open fire was retained, complete with original tiles and hearth. The grey chintz which envelopes the entire room has long been a favourite with the client, mainly because she finds it so tranquil in feeling but also because it seems so right for the architecture of the house. The bed-hangings are lined with striped silk, and the bedcover was specially knitted to a pattern for a baby's cot. The muslin-skirted dressing-table, antique furniture and patterned rug all sustain the country-house ambience.

The garden beyond

The decoration of fashion consultant Michael Reeves' flat was conceived as a background against which his collection of oriental objects would be given maximum account. Off-white walls, off-white carpeting and simple window treatments have been used throughout – except here, in the bedroom, where the windows are hung with festoon blinds. 'The garden outside was so green and fresh that I didn't want to cut it off, yet I wanted something different – something soft – as a contrast,' says Michael Reeves. He made the blinds in peach cotton overlaid with cream shantung and edged in lace. In order to achieve a sense of unity between the bedroom and the sitting-room (shown on page 80), the bed echoes the design of the seating. At its foot stands a group of oriental trunks – but the room's most important oriental element is the magnificent Japanese screen.

A room with powerful presence

Michael Szell is one of the most inventive fabric designers in Britain. His collections are always ravishing in their colouring and exuberant in their patterning, a demonstration of which can be seen in the vivid kelly-green linen decorating the bedroom of his flat in London. The room was designed largely round the collection of decorative oils which date from the sixteenth to the nineteenth century. He describes the method of hanging them as 'in the style of the studio of an eighteenth-century artist', but the informal impression given by this mixture of period and subject disguises the careful vertical alignment and overall use of wallspace. The linen wallcovering – repeated for the valance and dress-curtains – is of strong enough character to match the powerful paintings, gilt frames and light-wood furniture. The top bedcover is Bokhara silk.

An underrated choice

Because it is often described as a 'cold' colour, blue is underrated and under-used in interior decoration. Providing that the tone is right and that it is combined sympathetically with other colours, blue can provide a spectacularly successful background, especially for period furniture and furnishings, as can be seen in this bedroom in the South of France designed by Thomas Kyle. Any hint of coolness has been counteracted by the warmth of the yellow which lines and trims the window curtains and bed-hangings. The deep pelmets are especially notable for their swagged rope detail and gimped hemlines. The treatment of the bed canopy is repeated for the mirrored alcove housing a small sofa. And, at the window, there are two sets of curtains – blue 'dress' curtains and yellow 'pull' curtains – which take up the reciprocal colour theme. So, too, does the carpet.

Symbols of other times and places

This bedroom and adjoining bathroom are part of a commission for a flat in Paris in which the owner wished to use grand, eighteenth-century French furniture yet have an informal home without the doleful gallery-like quality so often associated with fine antiques. Jacques Garcia, the designer chosen to realize this challenging brief, has devised a series of rooms with great originality and vitality. In the bedroom, the ceiling has been painted in the traditional French manner to simulate sky and is

contained within a heavily-moulded and gilded cornice. Four lictor's fasces are basic to the masculine style of decoration. (Fasces, as every classicist knows, are those bundles of rods with axe-blades which were carried by Roman officers to carry out sentences meted out to offenders.) Billiard-table-green walls and curtains, antique rugs and military

furniture extend the masculine image.

The bathroom, which is treated in the manner of a small drawing-room, has a generously-upholstered sofa, braided curtains, an oriental rug and a handsome chandelier. The copper bath, lined with silver, continues the historical fantasy which permeates the apartment.

The trophies of taste

The breathtaking decoration and assured furnishings of this bedroom in Pennsylvania belie the fact that, only a few years ago, it was once a barn adjoining a farmhouse. The oldest part of the farm complex was built in 1720, but there have been many additions and changes since then, including Thomas Kyle's recent conversion of the barn into this summer retreat. Two bedrooms and two bathrooms were incorporated in the converted barn, plus a huge, airy living-room below (see page 204). In what is now the main bedroom, a Palladian-style window was inserted to echo the larger-scale window installed in the living-room. Then the wagon-vault ceiling was painted by André Dubreuil with flamboyant trophies and medallions within the architectural frames. The magnificent wallpaper with *trompe l'oeil* ruching and swags holds its own with the rich folds of the chintz hangings on the eighteenth-century bed. Ivory and bronzed pagodas stand on the table in the window seating-area, and a further Chinese element is added by the head-bobbing mandarin on the Italian gilded table.

A room-within-a-room

Chester Jones' parallel treatment of the bed and the walls in a Georgian house in London has created the effect of a room-within-a-room. The walls are covered with a warm-red cotton from Colefax and Fowler, which is also used for the window curtains. Within this outer layer of fabric, there is a second layer in the form of the bed-hangings in off-white cotton finished with red-and-ivory gimp and plain red braid. The window pelmets echo the undulating lines of the bed pelmet, thus counteracting any feeling of rigid rectangularity which could result from straight-edged pelmets. The room's colour scheme, though warm and inviting, is highly disciplined – as is the symmetrical arrangement of the lamps, decorative objects and paintings.

A calculated infusion of theatricality

Designer Mimi O'Connell abhors what she calls 'pompous' interior decoration but admits to being calculatedly theatrical at times. The bedroom of her own London home is a typical example of her confident style which combines flamboyant antique furniture and an ordered sense of colour. The extraordinary Venetian bed, with its barley-sugar posts and gilded finials, is casually draped with blue-on-white printed cotton suspended from a ceiling-mounted corona. Ribbon-pattern fabric in the same, fresh combination of colours is used to upholster the small button-back sofa. All the other surfaces in the room are plain – and mainly white. The double bands of blue paintwork on the walls, just below the cornice, are continued along the pelmet-board for greater symmetry and harmony. The surrealist painting, a surprising but effective element in the setting, is by Hector Borla. The circular table and chairs are Swedish 'Beidermeier'.

Sleeping beneath the sky

The impression conveyed by this pretty and secluded bedroom is that of a much-loved cottage – perhaps in Cornwall, perhaps in a village in the South of France. Its fresh and simple character is based on outdoor materials and themes – a paved floor, sky-painted ceiling, lilac-hung walls and, most important of all, a courtyard garden that seems to have become an integral part of the room's decoration. Surprising, then, to find that such tranquillity and floral plenty have been achieved in a basement flat situated in the heart of London.

Initially, the flat had the advantage of generous space and two patio gardens, but it was the imaginative eye of June Duprez, aided by Monica Pitman and architect Peter Crighton, that brought the place to life. Structurally, the biggest undertaking was to insert French windows onto the courtyards. The next major undertaking was relaying the shaky wooden floor. June Duprez was determined to imbue a sense of continuity between indoors and outdoors, and she spent considerable time and effort in looking for the right kind of tiles or marble. Eventually, she took the bold decision to use old York paving, and the results are exactly what she had hoped for. Whether the occupant of the room sleeps indoors or outdoors seems merely a matter of whim, for the two spaces appear interchangeable in function and decoration.

Using patterned fabrics to disguise plain walls

When Sabine Marchal was commissioned to refurbish a turn-of-the-century apartment in Paris, one of the major considerations was the preservation of the fine original cornices and mouldings. This was possible in all the rooms except the main bedroom from which every vestige of architectural interest had long since been removed. Rather than try to imitate the mouldings elsewhere in the flat, she decided on a completely different course which now conceals the room's unacceptable plainness with a series of co-ordinating patterned fabrics. The fabrics, which were specially printed, line the walls and ceiling, giving the illusion of a tent. This illusion is enhanced by strips of wall fabric being fixed along the cornice and diagonally across the ceiling. The bed-head is upholstered with a combination of the ceiling and wall materials, while the bed itself is overlaid with a Chinese cover of embroidered linen with lace inserts. The candle-lamps beside the bed were specially painted to ally with the fabrics.

The rural idyll

For city dwellers the country is a continuous yearning. 'When I get my dream cottage . . .' is the opening gambit of many a heartfelt discussion and totting-up of financial resources. No matter that friends' ventures into the cottage life have turned out to be fraught with problems, with damp and expense rising in direct proportion. The countryside and pastoral lifestyle exercise their invincible appeal, and no-one is daunted by tales of others' woes and misadventures.

The rural dream is constantly seductive and frequently misleading. The dream is always one of comfort and leisure with all necessary chores and labour concluded satisfactorily so that, with untroubled conscience, we can think self-indulgently of muffins for tea, an omelette for supper or a roast for the morrow. And often the dream is enacted in a country cottage, perhaps the most romantic of all dream settings, borrowing something from the Dordogne, something from the Cotswolds and something from New England, and assembling these elements into a captivating unity, all our very own. The windows will certainly overlook miles of unspoilt countryside; the table will most likely be stalwart, four-square and well scrubbed; the dresser will be well laden with decorative china; the tablecloth and napkins will be gaily patterned and coloured.

There may be a fire, and in the kitchen there will certainly be a stove ready for cooking and heating and for underpinning the general, genial ease which always, somehow, seems to pervade the rural home. Here is the most welcoming and romantic of settings, seemingly without a care in the world – and what could be more romantic than that?

Although the rural ideal permeates all areas of interior decoration, the desire that many city-dwellers feel for the country often manifests itself in the way in which they decorate those rooms in which food is of the essence: dining-rooms and kitchens. No one can fail to have noticed the renewed popularity of wooden kitchen units. It typifies the wish to associate with the past – a constantly recurring theme in neo-romantic decoration – but here it is touched by an idealized view of pastoral life. We *could* choose plastic laminate which looks unashamedly like plastic, but so often we prefer plastic which looks like wood – or, better still, real wood which looks like wood, knots and all. This preference for natural finishes and

A massive pine table is authentically rural in a rural kitchen by Janet Shand-Kydd. The cupboard treatment is equally and pleasingly un-urban.

Well-considered informality in a country-house dining-room is achieved by sun-yellow walls, pretty fabrics, patterned china and a paved floor. Designed by Janet Shand-Kydd.

(Opposite) A country kitchen which looks exactly as it should: natural, uncontrived and timeless. Designed by David Mlinaric.

(Left) Rush-seated chairs surround a generous table in a kitchen decorated by Pauline Mann. Meat dishes line the lintel above the inglenook. (Right) Wide arches, white walls and hefty beams are part of the vernacular in this airy sitting-room in Malta decorated by Penny Apap.

This dining-area of understated character combines many symbols of traditional country life in England. Designed by David Mlinaric.

(Left) A fruiting vine is painted on the stairway as a reference to the dining-area beneath. Designed by Sean Langton. (Right) The rural textures of oak beams and rush matting are juxtaposed with grand piano and fine bookcase in a hall decorated by Carrie Naylor-Leyland.

(Opposite) Expansive in area, reticent in design. A dining-room and kitchen in a rural conversion by John Stefanidis.

traditional forms has spread to kitchens throughout the Western world, the French having been particularly successful at exporting their *style rustique*. All those high-tech gadgets that chop, blend and extrude food within seconds are cosily and unexpectedly tidied behind Provençal-style cupboard doors, while the wall behind the streamlined hob is clad with rows of hand-painted tiles, often in Mediterranean patterns and hues. The tiles remind us of holidays, of time-honoured crafts, of farm-house simplicity . . . all nice, reassuring thoughts as we grab an instant breakfast in a boxy, urban apartment.

Interestingly, many new houses are being built with kitchens that are large enough for families to eat in, and estate agents make much play of the revived 'farmhouse-style' kitchen. 'A wealth of old beams' and 'a cosy inglenook' are not just advertising clichés but really do seem to reflect what people hanker after. Such is the craving for beamery and nookery that a whole new industry has grown up supplying glass-fibre and plastic 'beams' and 'bricks' to ruralize ceilings and walls.

But the really attractive characteristic of architecture and decoration with 'rural charm' – another term much loved by estate agents – is that it transcends social barriers. A 'rural' style of decoration in a grand house is never pretentious or intimidating, whereas an urban style, even in a quite modest house, is frequently affected and unfriendly. The kitchen/dining-room illustrated on page 164 illustrates this point very well. This is a large room in a fine house, and a great deal of thought and care has gone into achieving the appearance and atmosphere that it now exudes. Yet the room is warm and welcoming, more so than if it had been decorated in an obviously sophisticated fashion. The odd thing is that it would probably have been much easier, quicker and less costly to have decorated the room in a manner which, on the surface, would have looked twice as grand (but half as appealing). It requires singular skill to produce something as casual-seeming as this, but which is neither crude nor pastiche.

That sociable, familial room is in the heart of the country, but several of the other kitchens and dining-rooms illustrated here are pure *rus in urbe*. They may look very rural but their setting is distinctly city. The kitchen designed by Johnny Grey and shown on page 170 is in Hampstead but it could easily be in Hampshire. Johnny Grey was one of the first designers in Britain to break away from the all-melamine streamlining of the nineteen-fifties and 'sixties, and to re-establish a country, traditional look for kitchens. Now, many other designers and manufacturers are interpreting a similar preference for traditional values. One of the prettiest examples is the room designed by Elaine Wilson shown on page 168. This also combines a kitchen and dining-room but is reminiscent of a nineteenth-century American farm-house kitchen – somewhat idealized, perhaps, but that is what romanticism is all about□

Avoiding temptation

One of the problems inherent in converting cottages is the temptation to over-decorate. How many people have bought a cottage because they fell for its simple, natural charm, only to find themselves embarking on a disastrous programme of modernization which destroys the very qualities they admired in the first place! It takes understanding and self-restraint not to slide into the trap. The Earl and Countess of Dudley, whose holiday house in Devon started out in the

eighteenth century as two workmen's cottages and a lime kiln, have been very careful to retain the pleasing informality of the original architecture. Above all, a feeling of warmth, comfort and welcome pervades the house, an atmosphere due largely to Lady Dudley's skill in combining cherished objects from several previous homes with more recently acquired pieces. The rough stone walls of the sitting-room, painted in a pale yellow, are offset by the French toile curtains with a border of shells and other sea motifs. The sea, only yards away, plays an obvious role in the mood and style of the house, and this is reflected in the collection of sailors' valentine shell pictures and in the Victorian glass domes with sea-shell 'flower' arrangements.

English or French?

Although this room is in an eighteenth-century stone-built farmhouse in Sussex, it conveys much of the atmosphere of a rural interior in Provence – which is not surprising, perhaps, because its owner-decorator, Sabine Petit de Mirbeck, is French and has homes on both sides of the Channel. The room is dominated by the massive seventeenth-century oak refectory table which came from a monastery in France. The walls are painted in stippled ochre, a perfect colour to offset the large tapestry and several other pieces of French provincial furniture, including a Louis XV carved pine doughbin. The original stone floor and primitive painting contribute to the French mood.

An ideal retreat from the city

The city-dweller's romantic ideal of a weekend cottage must surely be along these lines: exposed beams, simple white walls, brick floors . . . but lots of comforts, too, in the form of well-upholstered seating, a mass of decorative pictures and objects, and efficient central heating. This charming room, decorated by Pauline Mann, is in a small Cotswold farmhouse built of gabled stone, with patched-and-thatched roof and leaded windows. When Pauline Mann bought the house, it was in a near-derelict state, but her imagination was caught by its underlying charm and she set about a sympathetic, low-key restoration. The result is an interior which is appropriately unpretentious but which reflects its owner's interest in art and antiques. The yellow-and-green Wedgwood plates, glimpsed through the doorway into the dining-room, were a London antique-shop bargain. The frames of the informally-grouped pictures are mainly of maplewood, the colour and scale of which are excellent foils for the character of the prints and country setting.

Rural but not rustic

With its immense Cotswold stone fireplace, exposed oak beams and leaded-light windows, the architecture of this room is unmistakably old and rural. But the character of the furniture and furnishings is more eclectic: a contemporary sofa and side-table are partnered by an early-nineteenth-century pedestal table and dining-chairs; and abstract watercolours are hung next to neo-classical figure paintings. The interplay of style and period was the outcome of the owners' brief to Lynne Comerford and Alison Billam of Top Banana Interior Design, specifying the inclusion of a number of existing possessions, many of which were modern. The age and country spirit of the house were in the forefront of the designers' minds when they began to work out their scheme, but these qualities had to be kept in perspective if they were not to overpower the new introductions. The designers have effected a balance between old and new, between restraint and comfort, by using palest terracotta distemper on the walls, simple lighting, no curtains, and by positioning the furniture to align with the fireplace and walls. This formal alignment is important in establishing a successful relationship between the vernacular architecture and the various pieces of furniture within it, all of which are sophisticated rather than rustic.

Memories of old Provence

The idea for this kitchen/dining-room in an eighteenth-century farmhouse in Gloucestershire was conceived many miles away, at the Colombe d'Or hotel-restaurant in St Paul de Vence in France. The owners were holidaying there with the room's designer, Lynne Comerford, who is a friend of long-standing and director of Top Banana Interior Design. When they saw the vernacular interiors of the hotel, they realized that these had exactly the timeless, homely feeling they wished to achieve in their country house in England. As their house is not a main residence, there was no need for a formal, separate dining-room, and they could see every advantage in having a room just like those in Provence which are truly the heart of home.

When the farmhouse was purchased it had been untouched for eighty or ninety years and it needed a great deal of basic work before the more enjoyable task of decorating could begin. This room, for instance, was originally four small rooms, and all the flagstones had to be taken up to insert a damp-proof course. Revealing the enormous fireplace was no less troublesome because it had been completely covered-in with a layer of plaster, behind which was embedded a Victorian range. The client wanted to keep the washing-up area away from the dining part of the room, so a half-wall was built at the back of the kitchen. All the hobs and sinks were set into old pieces of pine furniture, and these also serve to divide the kitchen from the eating-area. The Aga is an essential part of the room's function as well as decoration.

One of the subtlest yet most important means of creating the Provençal atmosphere is the 'distressed' paint finish and stencilling by David Mender, which have an authentic appearance of maturity.

Festooned with the colours of summer

If you were not told that this pretty dining-room, which doubles as a family living-area, is in Clapham, you could be forgiven for placing it firmly in the country. The colours, fabrics and general tenor of rural hopitality belie the urban setting and terraced architecture. The rooms were decorated by interior designer Marguerite Dewar-Durie and are incorporated in an extension to her own house which, although very much a family home – 'two young children and Cider, a large yellow labrador, can make their presence felt' – is also her business headquarters. When the Dewar-Duries moved into the house, the extension had already been built and the only structural alteration they needed to make was to enlarge the hatchway between this room and the adjoining kitchen. The furniture and furnishings were chosen for their sunny, 'farmhouse' character: a natural pine dresser, pine chairs, a big scrubbed pine kitchen table and an oak chest from Austria. The floor is a chequerboard of cork tiles.

Transatlantic cultural exchange

Elaine Wilson's roots are in America, where she was born and brought up, but her home is now in England, and her international design practice is based in London. Her love of old furniture, objects and paintings from both sides of the Atlantic is reflected in the interiors of a nineteenth-century townhouse in Knightsbridge which she recently refurbished with the technical help of architect Peter Brand. First modernized in the nineteen-thirties, the house was then rented

out for fifty years, during which time little or nothing was done to it. One of Elaine Wilson's first moves was to gut the basement in order to make an open-plan kitchen/dining-area. In the dining-area, which is separated from the cooking area by a white-painted wicker sofa, the fireplace is flanked by open shelves displaying a collection of spongeware and spatterware, amassed over about thirty years and made up of pieces found in England and the States. Elaine

Wilson's transatlantic collecting is also indulged by the naive painting, dated 1847, which hangs above the fireplace, and by the American stick-back chair alongside. To the right of the french doors to the garden is the original dumbwaiter lift to take food to the ground-floor dining-room. The room evokes an idealized American farmstead of yesteryear and charmingly expresses today's preoccupation with the simplicity of the past and of the country lifestyle.

A return to a friendlier style of kitchen

Johnny Grey was one of the first designers in Britain to break away from the all-melamine-look kitchen and to re-establish a friendlier, more traditional kind of decoration.

This kitchen/dining-room is in a long, narrow, two-stage extension to a mid-Victorian house in West Hampstead. As the extension was in a poor state of repair, there was a chance to replace the windows which were of uneven size and in unsuitable positions, and to redistribute them around a new interior plan. Johnny Grey's idea was to link the new window openings by creating a series of vertical open-storage buttresses to waist level, with caned seats between, and by

building a hanging rack at ceiling level which extends from these buttresses. This rack, acting like a false ceiling, also helps to break up the room's corridor-like proportions. Another bonus is the provision of high-level storage well out of reach of children.

The planning was otherwise kept simple: individual items of furniture were positioned to maximize efficiency of food preparation. The Aga sits in an old fireplace; the peninsula counter houses a fridge, back-up hob and granite slab for pastry-making. Each piece of furniture was designed to be stylistically self-contained, and the peninsula was influenced by 'thirties profiles – with a touch of artist's licence.

The stuff of magic

Not for a hundred years has there been such widespread interest in fabrics. The world's decorators seem to have rediscovered that passion, verging on obsession, which was so evident a feature of the high-Victorian home. Think of the Victorian mania for covering every table, piano and chairback with a cloth or shawl, and then consider the current fashion for the circular 'occasional' table with its floor-length cloth. As a rule, these tables indicate a feminine hand at work in a room's decoration, especially when they sport several layers of flowery cloths, all carefully co-ordinated and frilled. Male decorators tend not to be so addicted to the skirted table and, when they do use such a table, they show a much more vigorous taste in the choice of covering. This will usually be a single layer of theatrical fabric, possibly edged with a heavy fringe or braid.

The reasons for the popularity of tablecloths in Victorian times were, supposedly, a combination of responsible houswifery and matronly sensibility. The cloths were there to protect the surface of a valuable table and to conceal the legs which were considered suggestive. The latter reason is hard to credit, and it certainly cannot be the *rationale* for today's revival of this fashion. Nor can the wish to protect the tabletop be paramount as many of the tables which are now so clothed have been bought specially for the purpose and are made of such awful, cheap materials that their true identity should never be revealed. Why, then, are we surrounding ourselves by all these stuffs? The answer can only bring us back to the theme of this book – a wish to envelop ourselves with a romantic softness.

Another reason for the increasing use of fabrics in the home might be the close association between fashions in dress and in interior design. Dress fashions now change very quickly, and anyone who wishes to be in the avant-garde has to change his or her style of dress every few months. During the past twenty years, the home has also become a focus for our ability to keep abreast – or ahead of – fashion. There are 'fashion' colours even for such prosaic items as casseroles and bread-bins, but fabrics above all else in the domestic environment offer the home-owner the chance to show how he moves with the times. He may not be able to afford to change the carpet or the dining-suite every year, but he can swap the curtains, alter the pelmets, drape a Kashmir shawl over

Windows and walls in the same floral chintz gives an all-embracing sense of luxury in a dining-room in London designed by Anthony Little. The chairs are upholstered with a co-ordinating weave.

In this sitting-room in London, pink cotton prints are mixed and matched – one for the walls; another for the curtains, blind and sofa; and a third for the tented ceiling and Regency chairs.

(Opposite) The tall, narrow proportions of this small dining-room have been improved by the tent-like ceiling treatment, designed by Olive Sullivan. Printed moiré is used throughout.

(Left) To introduce a feeling of luxe into a small bedroom, Brian Juhos has upholstered the bed and ruffled the pillows. The windows have a double layer of co-ordinating fabrics. (Right) Close-gathered fabric ripples the walls in a breakfast-room designed by Samuel and Cooper.

'Cold' surfaces have been kept to the minimum in this bathroom in London. Instead, hot-coloured cotton is striped right across the walls and windows.

(Left) Fabric is a particularly sympathetic background for dining-rooms. Here, it is gathered across the walls, giving an even more cossetting effect. Designed by Ann Sheffield and Joy Arden. (Right) Chintz unifies bed, bedside tables and chair in a bedroom designed by Anthony Little.

(Opposite) An outdoor room designed by Gérard Bach and made entirely of fabric. Curtain walling is suspended from a vast umbrella of natural canvas.

the sofa, pile on the cushions . . . and thus give a room a completely new personality at comparatively modest cost. And he needs to do just that if he wishes to be seen to know what's what in interior decoration, for furnishing fabrics now date almost as quickly as dress fabrics. The patterns and colours, or combinations of colours, displayed in a room's fabrics can instantly give away the vintage of the room's decoration (and thus of the tastes of the owner) long before those fabrics are worn out.

Changes in the patterning and colouring of fabrics are matched by the way the fabrics are being used, especially for curtains and pelmets, which now show a marked harking-back to the eighteenth and nineteenth centuries. The shallow, straight piece of stiffened fabric across the top of the window, which was the standard pelmet arrangement in many a traditional room of twenty years back, now looks mean and out-of-date. Today's pelmets are much more extravagant – full, swagged and fringed. Throughout the whole of this book there are examples of pelmets which look flamboyant and confident, easily in tune with the nineteen-eighties yet derived from the eighteen-twenties. Even the curtains themselves are much more luxurious, often three layers deep. There are non-functional 'dress' curtains on the outside, then 'draw' curtains and, finally, voile.

But the ultimately self-indulgent use of fabrics is surely the tented room. This, too, was much favoured at the beginning of the last century and is enjoyng a revival. The availability of inexpensive fabrics and new techniques for applying them to the walls have undoubtedly aided its popularity. Not, one has to admit, that the tent-rooms illustrated here are based on inexpensive fabrics – but, nevertheless, with imagination and verve an excellent effect can be achieved using basic materials such as sheeting, lining and canvas.

The use of tenting can be a practical device for disguising poor plasterwork or improving proportions. The room illustrated on page 172 is a case in point. This arrangement shows how a long, narrow space with a disproportionately high ceiling has been made to seem cosier and more intimate by looping fabric from the ceiling to the walls along a line well below cornice level.

A tent-room of a particularly exuberant kind is the gorgeous example by Michael Szell on page 176. Given that Michael Szell is one of the world's most talented fabric designers, it is hardly surprising that he should use fabrics in such profusion. When you consider that he is also a passionate gardener, the whole floreated scheme falls into place, for here is the room of someone totally infatuated by fabrics and flowers.

Not all the rooms in this chapter display quite such a superabundance of fabrics as the tent-rooms, but they all use fabrics as the leit-motif of their decoration. In many instances, the fabric is fixed tautly across the walls as a softer alternative to wallpaper, but in some of the rooms the fabric is gathered to give a rippled effect☐

A decorative *melée*

Only someone who is obsessed by flowers and fabrics could have devised such a room as this. Textile designer Michael Szell is a keen and knowledgeable amateur gardener, whose hobby is a major influence on his professional as well as domestic life. This rose-filled tent, in which every surface is covered in blooms, is the sitting-room of his house in the West Country, a pink-and-grey belvedere designed by Robert Adam in 1769. 'The house has a façade which is perfection,' he says, 'but I wanted the interior to reflect my own more eclectic interests, such as this rose fabric which is based on my Prima Ballerina roses that grow so abundantly in the garden. I also incorporated all kinds of odd bits and pieces which I had picked up in the Portobello market and elsewhere, even some things which I had brought back from India. I think all these things and the fabric, which I made specially, make a mad sort of decorative *melée* which adds up to a marvellous visual pleasure every time I enter the room.' Within this *melée*, the arrangement of the furniture and objects is structured and symmetrical. Pairs of urn lamps, candelabra and mirrors flank the bookcase; two wing chairs align with the windows; elephant tables and tasselled sconces frame a shell seat.

An agreeable huddle

Although much of the furniture he uses is eighteenth century, decorator Henry Garelli wanted the sitting-room of this small apartment in France to have the weighty, huddled atmosphere of a room of the nineteenth century.

To achieve his aim, he has used lots of patterns, furniture and objects, all in close proximity. But the most significant element in his scheme is the pinch-pleated fabric which circumscribes the entire room. This hangs from a

brass rail just below the cornice but is not fixed at floor level, thus giving a felicitously free effect. The fabric is caught back to either side of the marble chimneypiece and, on the opposite wall, to either side a large panel of mirror.

How to be different yet the same

An assured use of fabrics and colour provides a link between this bedroom and adjoining dressing-room (right) in Italy. The designer, Adriano Magistretti, wanted the two rooms to be complementary to each other yet strikingly different, and the method by which he has achieved this parodoxical goal is silk damask, real and stencilled, in gorgeous shades of red and blue.

The bedroom was designed around the exceptionally handsome *Empire* bed embellished with flambeaux and upholstered with striped silk. The walls of the room are lined with red silk, and it was this fabric that inspired the treatment of the walls in the dressing-room. In the latter, the walls have been stencilled with a motif which is decoratively at one with that of the damask next door. The couch, or *dormeuse*, is covered with a soft-pink damask interwoven with threads of gold.

A room upholstered for visual warmth

This house in France was designed by François Catroux primarily for use in the autumn and winter. Thus, the finishes and fabrics in the sitting-room were chosen for their impression of warmth, a welcome attribute on cool evenings.

The dominant feature of François Catroux' scheme is the printed fabric which sports an eighteenth-century motif and has been used to line, drape and upholster all kinds of different surfaces. To restore the balance,

the parquet floor has been left bare, except for one off-white rug in the conversation corner (top left). This, together with the fabric-lined walls, defines the area and separates it from the rest of the room. Here, in an otherwise rather English-looking room, with comfortable sofas and wing chairs, one sees a French influence in the elegant white-painted Louis XVI-style chairs. The walls in the main part of the room have been painted with a special 'crackled' finish, the cornice and ceiling

mouldings highlighted in russet-pink, a colour derived from the handsome marble chimney-piece. Traditional furniture is a natural choice for a room of this character, and the eighteenth-century Provençal bureau and the small round mahogany occasional tables look well against the pale cream walls. There are relatively few accessories in the room, the principal interest being provided by the fabrics. An unusual detail is the pair of curtains which frames the mirrored overmantel.

Bathed in a rosy glow

This dining-room on the fifth floor of a Victorian block in Kensington, although spacious enough for a good-sized pedestal table and eight chairs, is too narrow to take additional pieces of furniture against the walls. If the walls had been left plain, the result could have been bleak and cell-like. To solve the quandary, Joanna Wood has softened the room's outline by covering the walls above the dado rail with shirred pink chintz. The dado has been stippled in pale pink which gives way to a darker shade for the mouldings and cornice. She chose pink for the colour-scheme because 'it is a wonderful colour at night. The room is bathed in a rosy glow, enhanced by candles and picture-lights which are ideal forms of dining-room lighting.' A co-ordinating pink-and-green striped chintz has been used for the festoon blinds and for the chair upholstery.

Images of the Arabian Nights

Combining a sitting-area and dining-area is fraught with difficulties in decoration. Too often these dual-purpose rooms look disjointed, disaffected and disagreeable. Alberto Pinto has resolved the problem in a comparatively small room in Paris by conjuring up images of the Arabian Nights. A co-ordinated pair of fabrics has been brought together with silk ropes and tassels to line the walls, curtain the windows and upholster the seating. By day, the cushioned banquette and stools face each other across low, X-frame glass-and-metal tables. By night, for parties, the latter are replaced by a cloth-covered table high enough for dining. Sparkling glass, china and cutlery accentuate the room's silken decoration reflected in the paired Venetian mirrors.

Recalling Africa and the East

This bedroom-cum-study and bathroom in a flat in Place des Vosges have been decorated by Gaston Bertholet with exotically-patterned fabrics recalling Africa and the East. The bedroom is all black and white, with zebra-styled walls and leopard-styled floor. Even the 'director's' folding chair in front of the black work-table continues the theme. A step to the right and you are at once transported to India by the kilim-inspired cotton in the bathroom. With full-length curtains, a small sofa and occasional table, a pretty chandelier, picture and bust, this delightful room has more the atmosphere of a sitting-room than a bathroom. Green and red are the dominant colours in the fabric and towels, and green is also seen in the marbleised surrounds to the bath and basin.

The spirit of the place

The poet and essayist E V Lucas came near to hitting a bull's eye as far as traditionalists are concerned when he said that the ideal domestic arrangement was to live in a Victorian house opposite a Georgian house, thus combining practicality, solidity and comfort at home with visual pleasures beyond.

But for many people the notion of living within a structure for which they have no sympathy or affection is wholly anathematic. For them, the structure itself and its associative qualities are every whit as important as the comfort and logic of the world within. For them, the *genius loci*, or spirit of the place, is everything. Hence the widespread passion for converted barns, warehouses, oast-houses, lighthouses, railway stations and redundant churches. There is something endlessly intriguing about living in a building which has had a previous existence. It engenders visions of all the past generations of inhabitants who have passed through the same doors and lived out their domestic or working lives in such very different circumstances.

At the outset, the main attraction of converting a barn, church or warehouse is the space and challenge that such buildings offer. They make quirky, individual homes which frequently provide at least one huge room, far bigger and grander than one could find in a conventional house. Furthermore, they do not conform to accepted ideas of domestic planning, thus not only testing one's imagination and skills in re-planning but having the potential to provide a home quite unlike any other.

The wish for space was what prompted artist Graham Rust to take on his old school-house in East Anglia. The main room is over thirty feet long, which was just what he needed for a combined sitting-room and studio (page 196). Space was also a major attraction in the conversion of a former fire-station in Philadelphia, shown on page 208. The lower floors have been used for more predictably-sized living-rooms and bedrooms, but the top storey has been turned into a spectacular sitting-room-gallery for an idiosyncratic collection of furniture and objects. Only an industrial or institutional building could have given such a magnificent and vast space, and the room makes triumphant play of the structural woodwork. The room on page 204 is also of vast proportions, but although the knowledge that it is a former barn undoubtedly adds to its charm, the style of decoration is

Vaulting and massive stone pillars bear witness to the early date and sturdy structure of Schloss Langenstein, a fortified castle in Germany recently restored and decorated by Gunilla Stanley for Count Axel Douglas.

(Opposite) An early eighteenth-century studio in Rome has been converted with artistry into a characterful flat. Designed by Dmitri Coromilas.

(Left) An attic dining-area in Paris, decorated by Robert Couturier in collaboration with Karla Entreprise, is defined by a huge beam and vivid red paintwork. (Right) An attic in Sussex has become a jolly bedroom for the children, designed by Sabine de Mirbeck.

Neo-bohemian dining-area converted by modern art consultant, connoisseur and collector, Stephen Reichard, from a loft in Soho, New York.

(Left) Teenage music-room carved out of the roof-space of a house in Hampstead. The quirky shape makes it all the more appealing. Designed by Gordon Lindsay. (Right) Architectural fragments decorate the stone landing at the top of the stairs leading to a flat above a fifteenth-century chapel in Rome converted by Jean-Pierre Rio.

(Opposite) Low, unobtrusive furniture was chosen in order not to detract from the seventeenth-century frescoes in a converted abbey in Tuscany.

far from rustic. It is a highly polished assembly of chintz and antique furniture, with only the exposed stonework walls bearing witness to its earlier life. The powerful character of the architecture remains, yet it has not inhibited the interior decoration. In contrast, the vernacular architecture of the Cotswolds barn shown on page 194 has been left bare and unadorned, and the massive stone walls are all-important to the room's character.

Not everyone, of course, is after huge, airy spaces. The intimacy of an attic flat with sloping ceilings and dormer windows is, for some, infinitely more appealing. They like to live way above everyone else and to feel cocooned beneath the roof. Perhaps they enjoy speculating on all those authors and artists who supposedly started their careers in tiny garrets, for there is still something vaguely bohemian and intellectual about living in an attic, with evocations of *fin de siècle* aesthetes discussing literature, art and life. Again, the force of the architecture is often seen as a challenge rather than as an impediment to interior design, as witness the major attic conversion shown on page 198 which uses the sloping roof to imposing effect. Here, part of the floor between the top storey and roof space has been removed, and the slope of the wall expresses itself through the double height.

The appeal of living in Tuscany, even in the tiniest of cottages, is obvious to all romantically-inclined souls. But to live in an ancient Tuscan abbey, surrounded by olive groves and vineyards, would surely be intoxicating. The foundations of the one-time abbey shown opposite could tell a tale that goes back over a thousand years. In 770 a man from Florence set out in search of a retreat where he could pray to God in peace and contemplate Nature. Seemingly blessed with a sixth sense, he went unerringly to the heart of Chianti, to an isolated valley surrounded by woods, its lower slopes ideal for vines. There he laid the first stone of the original abbey. That building is no longer extant, but some of the later additions, such as the twelfth-century bell-tower remain, as do numerous buildings of the fifteenth century, constructed on the plan of the convent of Saint Mark in Florence. Riches accrued during the sixteenth century resulted in frescoes in the refectory, now a sitting-room. Badia a Coltibuono, as the abbey is designated, is the home and headquarters of Piero Stucchi Prinetti, one of the most respected wine-producers in Chianti. He has painstakingly restored the building, but when it came to furnishing it, he felt that modern furniture of pure, uncomplicated shapes, would be the most appropriate style because it would not only be his contribution to the continuing tradition of the building, but it would not detract from the essential spirit of the place. The frescoes are so remarkable that he did not wish to introduce antique and decorated pieces which would have rivalled them. He also felt that simplicity was more in keeping with the building's earlier function□

Dramatic yet tranquil

The restrained grandeur and noble proportions of this interior might suggest a room within a medieval castle. In fact, the room is in a Cotswold stone barn, the exact date of which is difficult to pinpoint. Most Cotswold stone barns were built to a traditional design, frequently dating from the sixteenth century, though the main structure of this one probably dates from the mid-seventeenth century. The aim of the conversion was to create a striking and unusual house which would be simple and economic to manage with minimal help. A fundamental requirement, also, was to retain the structure in as unchanged a form as possible. To all intents and purposes this aim has been achieved and the building has remained as it looked in the days of King Charles. The huge main room – comprising hall, sitting-room and dining-room – is warm, functional and easy to run. The walls have been left rough, but now, instead of being filled with sheaves of corn, they have been hung with tapestries, antlers from Invernesshire and family pictures. A gilded Baroque looking-glass replaces bales of hay, and the floor has been relaid with paving stones which were retrieved from other Cotswold buildings; these have been burnished until they glow in a kaleidoscope of grey and ochre, russet and black. Sofas and leather-covered chairs – comfortably deep – provide sitting space; colourful rugs, and outsize dog-baskets (for outsize English mastiffs) lie about the floor. The two fireplaces – the only major additions to the living-room – seem permanently filled with blazing logs. The sparkle and smell of firewood and, perhaps, the soft whisper of a Bach or Scriabin sonata . . . the atmosphere is one of massive simplicity, at once dramatic and tranquil.

Once a school-house, now a studio

Artist Graham Rust's home and studio are in a converted 1870s school-house in a hamlet in East Anglia. It was built in 1870 and when it came up for sale in the 1970s, it seemed the perfect space for a studio, the main room being over 30 feet long and 16 feet high. In converting the school-house, Graham Rust built an interior balcony, the rail of which skilfully conceals one of the room's two ceiling ties. He then widened the chimneybreast by building false projecting walls on either side and replaced the cast-iron grate with a marble chimneypiece. The treatment of the chimneybreast is ingenious decoratively as well as structurally. Graham Rust had four blue-and-white pots which he thought would look well on brackets on the wall as a surround to the looking-glass – but he decided that he needed six for better effect. To that end he bought two well-shaped, plain brown pots and painted them to match the existing quartet. The bookshelves and *singerie* niche also emanate from the artist's brush.

A 'thirties attic with neo-thirties decoration

When decorator Frederic Méchiche was invited to renovate a two-storey attic apartment in Paris, he decided that as a decorative theme he could scarcely do better than take the nineteen-thirties building as the starting-point. And 'starting-point' is the *mot juste*, for the flat was originally a terrible muddle of small, dark rooms and mean corridors. Méchiche's first stratagem was to open up the interiors and to remove part of the upper-level floor to make bigger spaces and to let in more light. He has kept the links with the 'thirties and with the original attic atmosphere by using horizontal, tubular balustrading, Bauhaus-style rugs and chrome furniture, and by emphasizing the sloping wall which is now seen rising through both storeys. But if the architecture and much of the furniture are of the 'thirties, the way in which they have been juxtaposed with the occasional piece of eighteenth-century giltwood furniture and Egyptian busts is exuberantly contemporary.

Theatrical decoration in a lofty studio

This studio flat in Paris offered advantages and disadvantages in approximately fifty-fifty proportions. The lofty ceiling height and gallery were unusual and allowed scope for rather theatrical decoration. But the massive windows, although flooding the interior with light, were in danger of looking bleak. Then there was the additional problem in that the flat was rented unfurnished, and one of the provisos of the lease was that neither walls nor floor coverings could be altered, either structurally or decoratively. So the high white walls of the main living-area and the deep pink carpet were there to stay. 'These were not too difficult to incorporate,' says Nina Campbell, the English interior designer who redecorated the studio, 'but I was far more concerned with a second proviso imposed by the client: that none of the more permanent furnishings – curtains, for example – should be valuable enough to cause regret and nostalgia when it was time to leave the apartment.' Hence those pretty but inexpensive festooned curtains. These – all eighty-five metres – are made of the plainest of cream lining material which has been smartened up with dark red edging. The same cream fabric enwraps the chain support for the candelabra.

Beneath the gallery bedroom (see page 129) a painting by Roger Funt of Solzhenitsyn receiving the Nobel prize is flanked by a pair of tall candle-lamps (designed by Nina Campbell) and two lacquered cabinets.

Rising to the challenge

The structure of this small attic apartment in Place des Vosges in Paris, belonging to journalist Jean Madrolle, imposed challenging limitations on its interior decoration. The sloping walls in the main room (right) ruled out pictures, while the massive wooden beam visually cut the space in two. Jean Madrolle's solution was to turn the beam to advantage and treat it as the dividing-line between seating-area and dining-area, yet use a consistency of colour and decoration to ensure that the two ends of the room have a sense of continuity. He has kept everything very pale, very plain, in order to minimize any potential feeling of claustrophobia. Pattern and subtle colour are introduced in the fabric covering the pair of sofas which lap onto the pastel-toned dhurrie. The only heavy-looking textile is the Afghan rug beneath the glass-topped, trestle dining-table.

In the adjoining bedroom (above), a wall of cupboards is faced with tinted mirror for a greater illusion of space without the harshness of plain mirror. The other walls are lined with velvet.

The ultimate barn conversion

Converted barns seem to appeal to romantics world-wide – though few one-time farm buildings can end up looking quite so sophisticated as this one in America, which is part of an extensive farm complex owned by Thomas Kyle. A vast, round-headed window has been inserted at high level, and white-painted Chippendale-style balustrading used to define the new gallery and stairs. At the opposite end of the room, a marble fireplace has been inserted in the exposed stone chimneybreast. The colours of the furnishings reflect the room's function as a summer retreat: everything is bright and fresh, with lots of greens to pick up the garden views through the tall, ground-floor windows, and blues to echo the clement sky seen through the Palladian-style window and the skylights. The floor of local stone is new, but the rough walls reveal the original structure. The room has been conceived as a cool foil for the warmer-toned winter sitting-room in the main building (see page 24) and as a complement to the blue bedroom shown on page 142.

Above a sixteenth-century chapel

When visitors enter Jean Pierre Rio's apartment in Rome, they have to look twice, at least, to ascertain what is ancient and what is Rio-in-the-style-of-the-Ancients. Rio's interest in the history of the Roman villa is both academic and graphic, for in addition to his own researches he is frequently commissioned to make drawings of the buildings of antiquity and their architectural elements. His apartment in Rome, in which a number of his own paintings are hung, is in the attics above the chapel of San Tommaso de Cenci, built in 1522 adjacent to the *palazzo* of the Cenci family, one of the most important patrician families of the Middle Ages and the Renaissance. The long, narrow living-room of the apartment exemplifies Jean Pierre Rio's knowledge of classical culture as well as his mischievous approach to interior decoration. The mosaic above the fireplace may have the plausible air of some carefully preserved antique fragment – wavy at the edges and pieces missing here and there – but it was made by Rio himself, inspired by an eighteenth-century engraving, though many of the individual pieces originally embellished a villa in the Roman countryside. The room's diverse seating elements have been unified by plain white cotton, which is also employed for the Roman blinds and as a casual covering for a low table. The room is given further unification by the frequent introductions of terracotta-coloured textiles and objects, with touches of black for accents. All the decorative accessories – not least the picture by Rio seen on the wall at right – are architectural in spirit and/or shape.

Expressions of function and art

Looking like the inside of a great, upturned boat, this skeletal sitting-room was converted by George Brook Roberts from the top floor of a one-time fire-station in Philadelphia. Built in 1893, the fire-station was closed down in 1968 and, two years later, bought by designer George Doan as a home for himself and his extensive collection of antique furniture and objects. Apart from the sheer size and strangeness of the room, the spectacle is exaggerated by the unexpected juxtaposition of highly-finished furnishings with the rugged construction materials. The roof trusses, rafters and boarding have been left bare to express their function; so, too, have the brick walls. But all the things within the room display more sophisticated kinds of art and craft. Carving, gilding, weaving are represented by the French seating, Portuguese statues of angels and Portuguese needlepoint rugs.

The light in the shade

For many, not necessarily night birds, romance is a mood more likely to be sponsored after sundown than at dawn. For them, twilight is the moment when the whole world is transformed. Shadows are important to such sensitive appraisers of the domestic environment, and they have a passionate concern with the design, position and intensity of lighting: light is not merely illumination but the setting of a mood. 'Who wants to flood a sitting-room with light?' is their contention. They prefer carefully orchestrated pools of light and shade.

The truth is that rooms designed by enthusiasts for chiaroscuro *are* romantic in mood. Rude realism is put aside. Lighting is as much an element in the *mise en scène* as fabric or carpet. The proponents of such theatrical lighting are apt to apply their theories to every room in the house or apartment. Even in such functional spaces as kitchens, overhead lighting is taboo unless dimmed almost out of existence. A low level of background lighting is supplemented by directional lamps which play up (or down) the various elements in the room.

The bedroom is an obvious candidate for skilful and flattering lighting, but the sitting-room is where dramatic lighting is seen at its most persuasive. There are many people whose work timetable means that they rarely see their homes except in the evening. Virtually all their social life is conducted from twilight onwards, and thus it makes more sense to decorate their homes with that in mind. The dark green room on page 222 is a good example. The room was singularly undistinguished when it was built and it needed a strong line of decoration in order to become more interesting. As the owner intended to use the room almost exclusively in the evenings and for entertaining, there was no need for the decorator, André Dijan, to have second thoughts about using an umbrous colour on the walls. All those dire (and usually misguided) warnings about deep colours making a room look gloomy and smaller could be ignored; after all, the artificial lighting can be manipulated to 'adjust' the size and shape of the room as wished. André Dijan has positioned the lighting to make some areas recede visually (and thus make the room look bigger) and to give prominence to pictures which look almost as though they are suspended in space, free from the walls. The effect is highly dramatic and stimulating.

Glass designer and engraver, Dennis Abbe has deco-

Colour is minimal in this room designed by Claude Vicario. The walls and furniture look shadowy and dusky, as if seen at twilight.

The glossy brilliance of the walls and ceiling in this intimate dining-room in the Cotswolds, decorated by Lynne Comerford and Alison Billam of Top Banana Interior Design, looks especially effective in candlelight.

(Opposite) Reflected glory: a dining-room in Paris, designed by Frédéric Méchiche, in which every surface contributes to the room's elaborate sparkle.

(Left) Ceiling spotlights in a drawing-room designed by Derek Frost are focused on pictures and decorative objects for maximum evening impact. (Right) Mirrored doors and foil wallcovering shimmer beneath the light from the chandeliers in a hallway decorated by Anne Sheffield and Joy Arden.

White can be at its most dramatic at night – as in this dining-room in an eighteenth-century belvedere decorated by Michael Szell.

(Left) Lamps recessed in the post-modern entablature are directed onto Ionic capitals atop bookcases symbolizing columns. Designed by John Wright. (Right) A monochrome setting by Yves Taralon is especially dramatic at night when artificial lighting throws into relief the white sphynxes and painting against the grey wall.

(Opposite) Pools of light give dramatic emphasis to objects of grand size and shape. Designed by Sandra Cooke.

rated his New York flat (page 218) for ultimate enjoyment during the hours of twilight. As daylight fades, and the lighting is switched on indoors, the coal-and-flame-coloured interior glows with Jazz Age vitality.

If entertaining is an important part of your life, then lighting must be given top priority. Even the best-decorated room can be ruined by ill-considered lighting, while a nondescript room can often be retrieved by carefully-placed lamps and that indispensible decoration aid – a dimmer switch. Dining-rooms, especially, are likely to be used in the evening, and lighting is the most effective way to create a sympathetic mood. If it is a truly sparkling evening you are after – sparkling in all senses of the word – then the essential adjunct to lighting is mirror. Look at the room on page 210, which has the appearance of a many-faceted jewel.

Some rooms are night rooms because they could never be anything else. Take the one-room flat on page 216. This brilliantly executed design has been worked out within the old kitchen of a French mansion. Practically no daylight penetrates to the interior. Instead of doing the conventional thing and trying to catch whatever ray of natural light he could, the designer decided to turn the whole place in on itself and to create an introspective, all-in-one living-sleeping-dining-reading area. He introduced architectural ornament on an imposing scale because, using so much artificial light, he wanted the deep recesses of the dentilled cornice and mouldings to make forceful shadow patterns.

The approach to contemporary domestic lighting is now very much that of the theatre-set designer. The best modern lighting schemes undoubtedly owe a great deal to the theatre, cinema and even to magazines. The way in which rooms are lit for photography has had an enormous influence on everyday lighting in the home. To ensure that a room does not look 'flat' and featureless when it is reproduced in print, a photographer will often use highlights to give pools of intense light between areas of shade, thus establishing a sense of depth. The same is true of theatre-sets, where the lighting is contrived subtly to draw attention to a particular character or object which is significant to the scene. Interior designers have caught on to this, and they now use lighting to restructure a room, to play down the boring elements and to play up the good points. It often has little to do with function or safety – though it should have – but has everything to do with intangibles and fantasy. The room shown on page 220 illustrates the way in which 'professional' lighting expertise influences domestic design. It was arranged by Gaston Bertholet with assistance from David Massey, a photographer specializing in interiors. David Massey's skill in lighting for photography has undoubtedly contributed to the room's personality which is seen at its most compelling at night. Gentle overall light, interspersed with areas of brilliance and shade, creates a festive chiaroscuro for parties□

Decorated with vitality

The fact that this flat has been changed only slightly in well over a decade is a compliment to its designer, David Mlinaric, who now sees the interiors almost as a complete period piece. Although his client, a Canadian, has added to her collection of pictures and, occasionally, changed small pieces of furniture, the overall effect is very much as it was at the outset.

The flat is in a Victorian mansion block in Kensington but, in many ways, the style of the decoration is more North American than British: everything is always immaculate, arranged with flair and perfectly lit, yet there is nothing stiff, artificial or pompous about it.

When client and designer first saw the flat, they were agreed that no alterations should be made to the structure, nor to its architectural detailing. In spite of this traditional framework, David Mlinaric's scheme for redecoration was inventive and dramatic, using unusual colours, contemporary finishes and an eclectic choice of furniture. The single quality which now permeates the entire flat is vitality. The walls of the sitting-room are covered with a dark, textured linen, and the existing parquet floor stained charcoal-grey to match. Colour is introduced by a giant antique kilim and by the client's existing seating.

All in one room

Within the former kitchens of a Paris mansion, decorator Ortiz Cabrera has made an unique *pied à terre*, the style of which is at once modern and classical. Natural light has been deliberately obscured by black-painted shutters in order to give, first, privacy and, second, complete control of the artificial lighting to complement the owner's collection of books, pictures and objects. Thanks to a generous ceiling height, Ortiz Cabrera, who worked in collaboration with Jean Poubel, has managed to achieve a total flat, with ample storage space, within a floor area of only 500 square feet. As functional as it is comfortable, this one-room home comes into its own at night, when it provides a sympathetic and library-like atmosphere for the work, research and relaxation of an *amateur* of art. Three major design ideas ensured the success of the interior: the lavish use of mirror to create *trompe l'oeil* lighting effects; new architectural details, such as the heavy cornice, *oeil du boeuf* internal windows and the monumental chimneypiece, all of which help to 'build' the space; and, finally, the mezzanine balcony for storage. All the living-space is on the lower level, and everything there does double duty to make such a small room workable: the seating-area is also the dining-area; and the canopied bed (not shown) is disguised with a back-rest and cushions to provide additional seating.

A preference for twilight

The very best time to see this flat in New York is at twilight, when there is still a dusky hint of daylight outside but the lights are switched on indoors. Then, the translucent glassware, the rich reds and golden bronzes come into their own, and the mirrors, which play on the light and space from carefully chosen points in the room, further enhance those colours and surfaces.

The period that glass engraver and interior designer Dennis Abbé likes best is that brief Jazz-Age transition between Art Nouveau and Art Deco. His flat is filled with a remarkable collection of pieces – some, quite literally, found in the streets of the city – which are nicely balanced between light and dark, brilliance and reticence, opaque and transparent, almost as though the entire scheme were an opalescent René Lalique vase. The strange cast-offs which Abbé has picked up off the streets include the backdrops from one of Flo Ziegfeld's stage sets, the lights from the Roxy Theatre, some furniture, a fireplace and some mirrors. One of the backdrops is seen in the picture at left, now flanked by panels of mirror. In front of this are a pair of column lamps, an Art Deco mirror, a 'twenties statue of gilded terracotta and, in the foreground, a table made by Dennis Abbé recalling the engraved crystal of Lalique. The Regency chairs are some of the very few pieces in the flat which do not celebrate the Age of Jazz, but their black-and-gilt frames and ebullient upholstery are bold enough to cope with the theatrical setting.

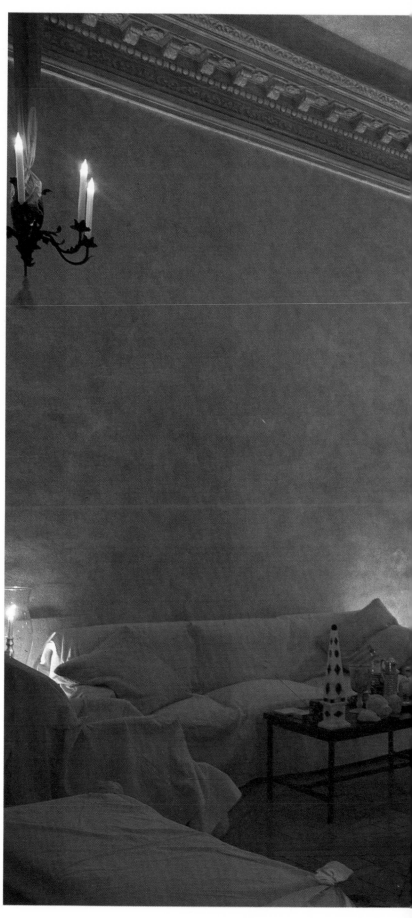

Arranged for a party

Creating 'atmosphere' or 'mood',
call it what you will, is one of the
most personal and difficult aspects
of interior decoration. David
Massey, who assisted in the
decoration of this fine 19-foot-
high room belonging to Gaston
Berthelot in Place des Vosges in
Paris, has an advantage in that he
is a professional photographer
specializing in interiors. He
knows the importance and
possible effects of lighting, and
here, when the room was set up
for a party, the real candles on the
table and realistic electric ones in
the chandeliers (which are
operated by dimmer switches)
give an overall glow punctuated
by brilliant dashes of sparkle. The
lurex cloth and silver tableware
give added highlights from their
reflective surfaces. Against a
background of sponge-painted
walls, the upholstered seating is
informally draped with white
cotton – a simple means of co-
ordinating sofas and chairs of
different shapes and styles.

For a nocturnal lifestyle

Very few recently-built rooms offer much in the way of architectural character and interest. This may be a sad reflection of a certain aridity amongst contemporary architects, but it is not always the hindrance to decoration that it might be. This room, for example, was totally blank and featureless when it was built – but that was just what challenged interior designer André Dijan and what gave him the perfect opportunity to instill his own particular brand of visual vitality. The two-part brief from his client was simple: make an impersonal room personal; and

design a room for use mainly at night. André Dijan has merged the walls and ceiling by using the same shade of dark green – velvet on the walls, lacquer on the ceiling – to compensate for the lack of architectural detailing and to give extra prominence to the works of art. The fine collection of drawings and prints is now brought into focus as a significant element in the room's decoration. The contrasts which are set up by the dark green background and the off-white sofa, blinds and floor, produce a lively visual exchange beneath well-considered lighting.

Old and well cherished

Twenty years ago, when many modern architects and designers were decrying high decoration for interiors, Geoffrey Bennison was busy creating rooms of startling richness and splendour. In the long term, Bennison's rooms have withstood the test of time better than the rooms designed by the modernists. This small attic flat in Soho was designed in the early 'seventies, yet it displays that well-cherished, lived-in-for-a-century look which is still a major influence on current interior design. Bennison's style was continually evolving but it was based essentially on the premise that beautiful things remain beautiful, even as they age, and that beautiful things of one period will live happily with beautiful things of another. Part of his skill lay in the unpredictable choice of objects, which were usually important in scale and form, and, of course, in their arrangement. This room is very modest compared with many of Bennison's later commissions but he has used bold furniture and patterns so that the treatment seems very grand. Lighting is also a major factor in this type of interior decoration. The room shown here was designed primarily for evenings, and the lighting was intended to accentuate the architecture and furnishings with dramatic highlights. Imagine the same room lit by conventional pendants with shades, and the result would not be the same thing at all.

The trellised bower

While we all admire the romance of raw, unfettered Nature when we travel in foreign lands – especially when we can arrive effortlessly by plane and stay in comfortable hotels – we like our home-based Nature to be tame and organized. Our gardens reflect the domestic wish for total domination of Nature, to the point where they are sad, stunted caricatures of the real landscapes we seek to emulate.

Indoors, we can get the best of all natural worlds in a conservatory. Here we can enjoy exotic, carefully controlled blooms all year round without the need for intrepid exploration in jungle or mountain. But even a sitting-room can be decorated in a manner which lulls us into thinking that we are communing with Nature. Indoor plants have become such a regular feature of interior decoration that we take them for granted, yet their prolific use and variety (and their low cost) are a phenomenon of our time.

Indoor plants have one characteristic which is especially useful in decorating a room – that is, they inject a living element where all else is static. This can often envigorate a rather colourless room in a way which, paradoxically, is restful and does not destroy the room's serenity. The introduction to an all-white room of, say, large-scale dark pictures would completely change that room from being white and light into being heavy and oppressive. The contrasts would be harsh and uncomfortable. But large plants, even with very dark leaves, will not change a room's essentially light character. Instead, they will emphasize the lightness while ensuring that it is not vapid or dull. One of the most stylish demonstrations of this is illustrated on page 232. The designer chose all-white for the room because he was commissioned to incorporate a collection of Indian and English silver. He was concerned lest so much glisten would prove an *embarras de richesse* if the room had lots of colour and pattern, but, at the same time, he felt that the room must not be bland. Plants are the method by which he has injected zest.

Another garden device which is being used increasingly in interior decoration is trellis. It gives an interesting effect when used as panels to divide, or semi-divide, a room, and it can be pinned on walls to create a courtyard look. Trellis can even be used to build a complete bower within a room – as in the example on page 230. This room posed quite an unusual problem – unusual, at least,

An ogee-roofed conservatory designed by Francis Machin makes a decorative and practical roof extension to a house in London.

In a house in Belgium, a floor-to-ceiling screen carved in wood (and backed by glass) allows glimpses of the indoor swimming-pool beyond. Architect: Serra di Mighi. Interior decorator: Christophe Decarpentrie.

(Opposite) This handsome entrance to an apartment in Paris, designed by Elie Garzouzi, is a synthesis of conservatory and hall.

(Left) Green-painted trellis gives added interest to the plain walls of a modern flat in Lyon and does not look out of keeping with the fine antique furniture and lacquered screen. It also makes a visual link between the seating-area and terrace. Designed by Carlos Ortiz Cabrara.

This airy structure, designed by Colin Childerley, combines the comfort of a conventional extension with the light and elegance of a conservatory.

(Left) A glazed extension designed by Christopher Coppack for an American publisher living in Chelsea provides a light-filled dining-area and kitchen. (Right) Brilliant blue and yellow glass, plus wicker furniture, are traditional elements in a new conservatory designed by David Garbutt.

(Opposite) Lace has been overlaid on trellis-painted walls in a neo-classically inspired room in Paris designed by François Catroux.

by today's standards of constricted living. The owners felt that the room was too big and bleak for dinner-parties: eight or ten guests seemed lost when they sat down in such a vast space. The solution was to erect an arbour in the centre of the room which gives diners a mild sense of enclosure without obliterating the overall sense of space, and to use carefully positioned lighting to accentuate the inner and outer areas.

Patrice Nourissat has gone to the other extreme in the converted warehouse on page 234. He has used every square inch of space, horizontal and vertical, for a jungle (albeit a highly organized jungle) of different fabrics, openwork balconies and masses of climbing plants. The effect is rather like one of those illustrations one sees of Edwardian conservatories with wicker chairs, fountains, jardinieres and stoves all placed hugger-mugger beneath a soaring glass roof and with plants invading and trailing from all sides.

Plants and trellis are also the theme in the hall shown on page 226. The space is large and elegant, suggesting from the outset something more than just a traffic-route between front door and sitting-room. Hence the hand-some console table and chequered marble floor in the traditional mode for a grand entrance or orangery. The window is screened by a folding screen which, appropriately, has panels of trellis, and by dramatically-lit plants. The gardenesque impression is underlined by the wicker seating.

The room illustrated on the opposite page conveys an equally conservatory-like quality, though it is in the heart of Paris. Designed by François Catroux, it uses many skilful devices to achieve a balanced, classical harmony. The walls were originally covered with an-tique trellis-patterned paper which, though no longer attractive, had to be retained because of its age and uniqueness. François Catroux' solution to the decoration problem posed by the paper was to overlay it with fine lace so that the paper is partially obscured, showing through just sufficiently to be decorative. The lace has been fixed to the walls in a manner that enables it to be removed without damage to the paper. The 'marble' floor is in fact carpeting, designed by Catroux, which has the dual benefits of looking suitable for a conservatory-like interior whilst providing the softness and warmth required for a year-round sitting-room.

A conservatory par excellence is that belonging to Nor-man St John-Stevas and shown on page 238. Norman St John-Stevas has always been fascinated by buildings and when he moved into his 1837 terraced house overlooking a London square he decided to build a conservatory in the Strawberry Hill gothick style (of which he is particularly fond) in order to bring a greater sense of space and light to the existing house as well as to provide an agreeable extra room in its own right. He describes the conservatory as a 'Knightsbridge folly': a suitably picturesque description for a romantically-designed room□

A pleasant sense of enclosure

Space is undoubtedly a luxury, but too much of it can be intimidating, especially in an age when we have become accustomed to scaled-down rooms with low ceilings, and to bland, simple forms of furniture and decoration. In older houses, if you do not wish to decorate the rooms in period, the tall proportions can be difficult to cope with. In this instance, a vast dining-room in France, decorator Chouchane Romeo-Pennes and architects Studio Enca have got round the problem by designing a free-standing trellis arbour which gives guests a diaphanously pleasant sense of enclosure. The window of the room is screened by plain blinds at night and by a curtain of plants during the day. Artificial lighting from overhead spots and uplighters positioned outside the arbour, all operated by dimmers, makes pretty and varied patterns when filtered through the trellis. The garden-like quality of the setting is played up by the exposed brickwork of the perimeter walls which have been painted white.

Like a white-and-silver sari

Sparkling yet discreet, brilliant yet restrained, this room reminds one of a beautiful sari of white silk embroidered with silver. In order to temper all the gleam of the client's unique collection of English and Indian silver, and in order to avoid turning the flat into a museum, Elie Garzouzi decided on two main courses for his decorative scheme. First, he has excluded all strong colours and, second, he has introduced large and numerous plants to bring an element of naturalness to a highly sophisticated setting. So much highly worked silver and rich fabrics could have appeared too much of a good thing, but everything has been so carefully and airily distributed that each piece can 'breathe' and does not detract from its neighbour. The trellis panels maintain the room's overall sense of spaciousness while subtly dividing what is an extremely large area into two smaller, more intimate spaces. The panels at left project partially into the room; the panels seen at right are fixed against the far wall, which is mirrored on the part nearest the window.

From workshop to plant-house

Difficult to imagine that such an indulgent-looking interior, decked out with swagged fabrics and cascading plants, was once an industrial workshop. The original workshop, like many others in the Marais quarter of Paris, had been slotted in between and behind two fine, early houses. It did not have much to offer in the way of architectural beauty – but it did have space, lots of it, which was just what Patrice Nourissat had been looking for. He has kept the sense of openness but added a decorative balustrade to the gallery and inserted a coffered wooden ceiling beneath it. He also kept the open fireplace but added columns, a portrait medallion and mosaic to turn it into a monumental, classical focal-point. The wooden floor was retained but painted with an 'optical' pattern. The vast area of glass overhead and the big windows had advantages and disadvantages – lots of light to feed the plants but too much glare for human comfort. The solution has been to use taffeta festoon blinds at the windows and to loop a billowy awning of striped cotton beneath the skylights. In fact, the lavish use of fabrics is a key element in the room, for almost every chair is upholstered in a different colour or pattern. Paradoxically, there is nothing jarring about this interior – it all seems mildly chaotic yet very much of a piece.

Tranquil colours and patterns

In a spacious, multi-purpose living-area designed by Francois Catroux, screens of slatted wood, painted to simulate ivory, are used as shutters as well as to form intimate seating corners and a dining-area. Between the screens and the windows are silk blinds in the same shade of ivory. A limited range of soft colours and homogeneously geometric patterns results in a setting of utmost tranquillity. Lots of plants and flowers are essential to the room's conservatory-like atmosphere which is in marked contrast to the urban view beyond the balcony.

A weakness for Strawberry Hill gothick

Norman St John-Stevas' house, in a central London square, was built in 1837, but the inspiration and ambience are far more Regency than Victorian. The house is tall and narrow so he has made it appear more spacious with an expansive back hall and a conservatory at the top of the first flight of stairs. The approach to the conservatory is through glazed gothick doors flanked by lifesize gilt busts of Queen Victoria and Prince Albert. The conservatory, which Norman St John-Stevas terms his 'Knightsbridge folly – inspired by thirteenth-century French Perpendicular', indulges his weakness for Strawberry Hill gothick. Stuffed pheasants line the entrance and plants vary with the season: camellias in winter: jasmine and plumbago in spring: bougainvillea in summer, and geraniums all year round.

The nautical fantasy

We all know how vistas can contribute as much to the ambience of a room as furniture, books and pictures. A less tangible contribution, perhaps, but one that is recognisable and acknowledged.

Most of us can recall the excitement of crossing to the window of a room in an hotel or a friend's house and looking out upon a scene which prompts immediate visual pleasure: across fields, towards mountains, above the seashore. Instantly, the room we are in becomes that much more interesting and appealing. The contents may be less than exciting, but the room remains in the memory as a romantic shelter. Undoubtedly, the most stimulating and awesome of all vistas to enjoy from the security of such a shelter is the sea.

The best and most sensitive architects always know when and how to play up the most important features of a house or flat. Dennis Wilcut got things absolutely right when he made sure that the unique view seen opposite and on page 244 was treated as the focal-point for the entire decoration of the house. He turned the whole scheme on the view and rearranged the existing architecture so that there was an uninterrupted outlook from the main rooms. The bedroom windows were extended from wall to wall and a platform was built for the bed so that the owner can wake up and look straight out to the beach and ocean beyond. He even installed electrically-operated curtains so that, at a press of a switch, they can be drawn back, theatre-like, to reveal the panorama.

In another beachside house in America, shown on page 252, the designers have decorated with the colours of sand because they wanted to blur the barrier between indoors and outdoors. They used simple, natural materials, all in shades of beige – with occasional touches of blue and white to pick up the colour of the sky and sea. The utter simplicity and appropriateness of the interior decoration is curiously romantic in a setting of such natural splendour.

The sea is also the theme of the decoration in the holiday house on the Italian island of Elba on page 250. Here, the main sitting-room is decorated with natural materials and embellished with objects with a nautical theme. Shells, a flying fish and swordfish blade all contribute to the decorative cross-referencing between interior and exterior. The fact that the house backs onto forests is represented, metaphorically, by the staircase in the form

The ultimate nautical fantasy: a 140-foot schooner built around the traditional Greek caique hull. Meals can be taken out on deck beneath a canvas awning spread over the boom. Designed by Jon Bannenberg.

(Opposite) Ultra-sophisticated version of ideal holiday-house decoration: light colours, clear patterns, natural flooring – and a fine outlook. Designed by Dennis Wilcut.

Twin cabins with twinned decoration by Vivai del Sud. Good functional design ensures that every inch of space is used efficiently, but practicality has not ruled out decorative colours and fabrics. Both cabins look appealing and 'work' effectively.

In the incomparably romantic setting of the Villa San Michele on the island of Capri, a sphynx gazes out to sea from the covered terrace.

Lakeside house designed by Hugh Newell Jacobsen for Warren Katz in Virginia. The living-room opens onto a deck with boats moored alongside.

(Opposite) An impressive shell sculpture symbolizes the seaside setting of this holiday house in Italy designed by Marika Carniti.

of a tree. The trunk, which forms treads and risers, is made up of thin horizontal layers of wood, and the branches twine their way up the walls and across the ceiling between the beams. Marine metaphors and natural materials are again the themes in the Sardinian house illustrated on page 246. Throughout the interior there are frequent allusions to the sea, mainly in the form of huge wallpanels of canvas painted to resemble billowing sails and roped to wooden frames, which not only establish the holiday function of the house but create an individual and memorable scheme of decoration.

Less natural in its use of materials is the flat, also in Italy, shown opposite. The finishes are smooth and sophisticated, but the arrangement of the built-in furniture funnels the eye towards the terrace and the view of the bay beyond. The terrace and living-room are designed as one interflowing space so that, in summer, there is no obvious distinction between the two.

But these are all rooms on *terra firma*. A good case could probably be made for the contention that the most thrilling of all sea vistas are those to be obtained from the saloons of the ocean-going yachts of the international well-heeled. One day, St Trop, another Portofino, and so on. (Not that the seagoing notions of such moguls are especially romantic when compared with the ventures of David Scott Cowper, Sir Francis Chichester, Robin Knox-Johnston – and other single-handed world girdlers. Far from it!)

These craft of the rich have what ninety-nine per cent of the world's yachts so emphatically lack: space below decks. A saloon in a tycoonish ocean-going yacht, by an international marine designer such as Jon Bannenberg, could, for example, be some thirty feet by twenty, and possessed of the wide windows of a penthouse. No longer those eyeglass portholes of yesteryear.

The interior design of yachts is a fascinating study. The ingenuity required to make every inch work and to combat all the problems encountered during the rigours of sea-going provide many lessons for designers working on schemes for small spaces on dry land. The galleys and shower-rooms of yachts are invariably brilliant exercises in function and planning, way outshining the level of design seen in tiny kitchens and bathrooms in flats and bed-sitting rooms. And sea-going saloons also demonstrate that function and efficiency are not synonymous with aridity in decoration.

Other craft of more modest dimensions and specifications can still offer scope and challenge to the interior designer. A houseboat, for example, also needs to be well planned if it is to provide a full-time comfortable home which is possessed of just enough 'salt' to maintain the nautical fantasy. The boat shown on page 254 may be moored permanently in Chelsea and designed along the lines of a conventional flat but, nevertheless, the structure of the hull inevitably means that the romantic associations of living on-board-ship are well in evidence□

Designed for barefoot living

The best designers let special features of a house speak for themselves. In this seaside retreat on the West Coast of America, the outdoors was paramount, and all the structural alterations and decoration were geared towards its enhancement.

Designer Dennis Wilcut removed the wall between two small bedrooms upstairs to make one long 40-foot space. Then the two ocean-side windows of the new room were bridged by a panel of glass to give a wall-to-wall vista of the terrace and sea. Finally, a platform was built to raise the bed a few inches off the

floor – just enough for the client to see the ocean from the bed. To dramatize the enjoyment, the curtains can be opened, stage-like, at the press of a button. Behind the Wilcut-designed bed, the lacquered bifold screen is stencilled with a stylised chrysanthemum, an oriental symbol of life.

'All the textures and surfaces in the house echo the look of the beach,' says designer Dennis Wilcut, '. . . sisal flooring, cotton upholstery, with plants and flowers the only accessories. Furniture is deliberately simple so as not to detract from the view.'

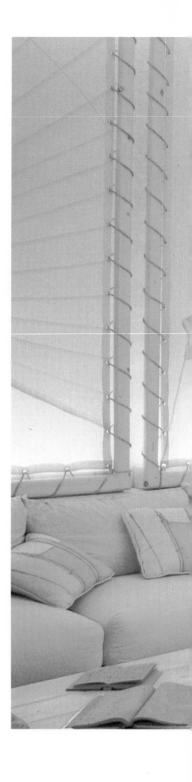

Marine metaphors painted on canvas

Marika Carniti's scheme for the interior decoration of this house in Sardinia was motivated by the magnificent and unspoilt coastal setting. Rocks, sand and sea have all played a part in determining the colours and rugged simplicity of design. But even more to the point are the frequent allusions to sailing, which not only underline the holiday function of the house but have become decorative features in their own right.

The effect of the interiors is almost surreal: visitors have the feeling of being at once separate from, yet totally part of, the seascape. The sensation is that of being swept along in an immaculately-detailed yacht. This has been effected by the wall panels of natural canvas, painted to resemble huge billowing sails and roped to wooden frames. The luminosity of the giant sails is emphasized by their being lit from behind.

Panorama on the Pacific

Greenhouse-style windows capture the light and view in a house set in a private cove, just an hour from San Francisco, with conifer-rimmed hills, tame surf and soft wind blowing through the sea-grass. It was designed by John C. Walker of Walker & Moody for Joseph and Jane Flahavan who wanted 'a simple, stark house' that would amply accommodate friends and festivities. In the lofty room for living and dining, Jane Flahavan's wicker-and-sailcloth scheme is a complete change from the silks and oriental carpets of their city apartment. The house has many reminders of sojourns abroad: from Italy, a white market umbrella on the terrace; from Hawaii, yellow patchwork cushions. The room's colours, says Jane Flahavan, 'are all those of Monet: blue, white and yellow.'

Indoor nature

Nature seems to have taken over in this holiday house overlooking the harbour at Porto Rotondo in Elba. The living-room is dominated by sculptor Ascanio Palchetti's tree-form staircase, in which the 'trunk' is the steps and the 'branches' extend up and across the walls, twining their way between the beams of the ceiling. The tree theme is a response to the wooded landscape behind the house, while the marine objects on the table, the swordfish 'obelisk' on the chimneypiece and flying fish which arches so dramatically above the sofa, are all appropriate rejoinders to the seascape beyond the terrace.

Less means more

Are those views of the dunes and sea, seen in the photographs below and at right, real or are they hyper-realist paintings? One cannot help wondering, because the ultra-simple architecture of the windows, left without curtains, allows Nature to enter the room so freely that the impression is that of a series of frescoes. The house is on a beach at South Hampton, a seaside resort near New York, and was completely restructured by Bob Patino and Vicente Wolf. Simplicity, practicality and harmony are the *rationale* behind the quiet but eloquent scheme. The exterior was refaced with natural cedar, and the interior decorated with the colours of sand.

Living in a saloon

Interior designers Chris Davies and Martin Bass normally specialize in schemes on *terra firma* but, in this case, they joined forces to transform a Thames house-boat which had seen better days into a comfortable home. After structural work had been carried out – the dividing door in the living-area, the light-obstructing hatch and the galley-stairway were removed – Davies and Bass set about doing their own painting and decorating. Their primary objective was to create a sense of space with maximum light, so they reduced clutter to a minimum. The long saloon is some twenty-five feet by fifteen, with high-level windows, a potentially austere space which has been made more attractive by Indian-cotton covered sofas, cream-painted plank-on-plank walls, Berber carpeting, plus two seating units upholstered with an abstract pattern cotton. Two antique decoy ducks and a group of china bowls, all in white or palest off-white, decorate the low, stipple-painted table. Existing spotlights were removed and replaced by more discreet downlighters.

Acknowledgements

Jacques Bachmann 5 (top row far right and bottom row centre right), 15, 50 (top left and centre), 72–73, 78–79, 82, 86–87, 88–89, 90–91, 92–93, 96–97, 103, 116–117, 140–141, 150–151, 175, 178–179, 182–183, 186–187, 192 (top left), 193, 198–199, 210, 212 (bottom right), 216–217, 222–223, 226, 227 (bottom), 228 (top left and top right), 230–231, 232–233, 234–235, 236–237, 256 (top row centre left and bottom row far right); Jon Bannenberg 241; Emmett Bright 11, 26–27, 70–71, 76–77, 119 (top), 180–181, 190, 242 (centre); Richard Bryant 60–61; Henry Clarke 28–29, 114–115; Alan Dovifat 208–209; Chris Drake 84 (top left), 172; Michael Dunne 16 (bottom), 50 (bottom right), 67, 84 (bottom right), 94–95, 98–99, 104 (top right), 120 (bottom left), 173 (top), 174 (bottom right), 256 (bottom row centre right); Andreas Einsiedel 18–19; Clive Frost 3 (bottom right), 5 (top row centre right and second row far right), 12 (top), 14 (bottom), 34–35, 65, 66 (top left, top right, centre and bottom left), 68–69, 74–75, 84 (bottom left), 104 (centre and bottom left), 136–137, 154 (top left), 160–161, 176–177, 212 (top left, centre and bottom left); Isodoro Genovese 40–41, 242 (top left and top right); David Glomb 121; Roberto Granata 20–21, 243; Jonathan Green 227 (top), 228 (bottom left); Pascal Hinous 12 (centre left), 62–63, 229; Ken Kirkwood 5 (bottom row far left); 13 (bottom), 196–197; Russell MacMasters 248–249; Gerard Martinet, 85, 122–123; David Massey 3 (top left and bottom left), 5 (top row far left and second row centre left), 10, 12 (centre right), 13 (top and two centre),

14 (two centre), 16 (top), 22–23, 24–25, 30–31, 32–33, 36–37, 38–39, 47 (bottom), 54–55, 58–59, 66 (bottom right), 83, 108–109, 110–111, 124–125, 128–129, 138–139, 142–143, 174 (top left), 184–185, 188–189, 192 (centre and bottom right), 200–201, 202–203, 204–205, 206–207, 211 (top), 220–221, 242 (bottom left and right), 256 (top row centre right); Norman McGrath 252–253; Duncan McNeill 154 (top right and bottom left), 228 (bottom right); James Mortimer 5 (top row centre left), 9, 14 (top), 16 (two centre), 44–45, 46, 56–57, 64, 102, 112–113, 120 (centre), 144–145, 152, 154 (centre), 155, 158–159, 174 (top right and bottom left), 192 (top right), 212 (top right), 214–215, 224–225, 256 (top row far right); Marina Papa 246–247; Karen Radkai 12 (bottom), 100–101; Fritz von der Schulenburg 3 (top right), 5 (middle row far left and centre right, bottom row centre left and far right), 17, 42–43, 48–49, 50 (top right), 51, 52–53, 84 (top right and centre), 104 (top left and bottom right), 106–107, 118, 119 (bottom), 120 (top left, top right and bottom right), 126–127, 130–131, 132–133, 146–147, 148–149, 153, 154 (bottom right), 156–157, 162–163, 164–165, 166–167, 168–169, 170–171, 173 (bottom), 191, 192 (bottom left), 194–195, 211 (bottom), 213, 228 (centre), 238–239, 254–255, 256 (top row far left, bottom row far left and centre left); Tim Street-Porter 105; Studio Azzuro 218–219; Tissunique 174 (centre); John Vere Brown 80–81, 134–135; Peter Vitale 6; Miussy Werner 250–251; Charles White 240, 244–245; Peter Woloszynski 47 (top), 50 (bottom left).